Romania:
The Entangled
Revolution

THE WASHINGTON PAPERS

. . . intended to meet the need for an authoritative, yet prompt, public appraisal of the major developments in world affairs.

President, CSIS: David M. Abshire

Series Editor: Walter Laqueur

Director of Publications: Nancy B. Eddy

Managing Editor: Donna R. Spitler

MANUSCRIPT SUBMISSION

The Washington Papers and Praeger Publishers welcome inquiries concerning manuscript submissions. Please include with your inquiry a curriculum vitae, synopsis, table of contents, and estimated manuscript length. Manuscript length must fall between 120 and 200 double-spaced typed pages. All submissions will be peer reviewed. Submissions to *The Washington Papers* should be sent to *The Washington Papers*; The Center for Strategic and International Studies; 1800 K Street NW; Suite 400; Washington, DC 20006. Book proposals should be sent to Praeger Publishers; One Madison Avenue; New York, NY 10010.

The Washington Papers/152

Romania: The Entangled Revolution

Nestor Ratesh

Foreword by Edward N. Luttwak

Published with The Center for
Strategic and International Studies
Washington, D.C.

Westport, Connecticut
London

Library of Congress Cataloging-in-Publication Data

Ratesh, Nestor, 1933–
    Romania : the entangled revolution / Nestor Ratesh.
        p. cm. – (Washington papers, ISSN 0278-937X)
    Includes bibliographical references and index.
    ISBN 0-275-94145-0 (HB). – ISBN 0-275-94144-2 (PB)
    1. Romania – History – Revolution, 1989. I. Title. II. Series.
    DR269.5.R38 1991
    949.803 – dc20   91-18244

The *Washington Papers* are written under the auspices of The Center
for Strategic and International Studies (CSIS) and published
with CSIS by Praeger Publishers. The views expressed in these papers
are those of the authors and not necessarily those of the Center.

British Library Cataloging in Publication data is available.

Library of Congress Catalog Card Number: 91-18244
ISBN: 0-275-94145-0 (cloth)
        0-275-94144-2 (paper)

First published in 1991

Praeger Publishers, 88 Post Road West, Westport, CT 06881
An imprint of Greenwood Publishing Group, Inc.

Printed in the United States of America

∞™

The paper used in this book complies with the Permanent
Paper Standard issued by the National Information Standards
Organization (Z39.48-1984).

10 9 8 7 6 5 4 3 2

To the memory of
Vlad Georgescu,
scholar and dissident,
forerunner of the
Romanian Revolution

Contents

Foreword

Once upon a time there was Eastern Europe, a rather homogeneous presence of which we knew a great deal. All its policemen and soldiers wore sub-Soviet uniforms; all its economies were crippled by the original sin of central planning, aggravated by costly industrial ventures of huge dimensions and minimal efficiency; all its automobiles were curiously outdated; all its rulers were subservient to Moscow; and all of its territory belonged to that extension of Soviet power known as the Warsaw Pact. As for its politics, they were of a kind too—the politics of repression, conducted by execution in the first postwar decade, imprisonment in the second, and censorship and exile thereafter.

In truth this uniformity was already compromised more than a generation ago, when national-Communist and then plain national identities began to variously reemerge. But it was not until the wonder-year of 1989 that "Eastern Europe" suddenly and totally dissolved, to reveal the fully formed lineaments of complete countries that indeed had very little in common and about which little is known. For that finally is the ironical result of an imposed Communist homogeneity under Moscow's uniform suzerainty. From Portugal to Sweden, from Scotland to Greece, ancient differences are now overlaid by a common Western interpretation of modernity in all matters from democratic politics to popular tastes, but the common Sovietizing patterns of modernity were everywhere so well resisted that the former East Germany and Bulgaria, Poland and Romania, even adjacent Hungary and Czechoslovakia, retained fully separate identities in every respect.

Of these identities, the Romanian is by far the most complex and also the least known except for Bulgaria's. Prewar Poland was a congerie of peoples but is now overwhelmingly Polish, as Hungary is almost completely Magyar; Czechoslovakia is split by its two main nationalities, and Bulgaria has its oppressed Turks. But only in Romania is the nationality-ethnicity split present even now in its full virulence, because only there a large (Hungarian-speaking) minority remains unreconciled to national rule—just as only in Romanian towns can one still overhear locals speaking four different languages around one market stall (German, Hungarian, Romanian, and Romany, along with Serbian or Ukrainian in places). At the same time, nothing has intervened to moderate the full-bore nationalism of the ethnic Romanian populace, whose fiery sense of exclusive nationhood retains the pristine quality that was once encountered everywhere in Europe, but which is only a memory in, say, Italy, and is now dulled even in Poland.

That, however, is the least complex of Romania's complexities, a mere matter of statistics. Far more intricate are the antecedent, pre-independence influences that still weigh heavily in Romania's governance. Austro-German antecedents still have their influence in Hungary and Czechoslovakia, just as Russian and German antecedents influence Poland, not to speak of the uniformly German antecedents of ex-East Germany, and Bulgaria's unalloyed Ottoman history. But only in Romania are all those antecedents represented in the collective memory, fragmentary bureaucratic practices, and everyday habits, along with a language that still preserves the rude Latin of the auxiliary troops and legions of the Roman army, and a far more sinister tradition of unique misrule, now being unconsciously perpetuated by the present rulers of Romania.

That is the tradition of the Phanariots. Now forgotten, those Greek tributary rulers, whose name recalls their provenance from the Lighthouse (*phanar*) quarter of Constantinople, were once well known in Europe as the very exemplars of misrule. The Mavrocordato, Ghica, Callimachi, Ypsilanti, and Murusi among other families, aspired to the culture of Byzantium and cherished their recitations of Homer, but derived their power from the Sultan. The Ottomans have an evil reputation but their taxation was not extortionate. The Phanariots, however, rented their rule by fixed payments in advance and, having no security of tenure, had no reason to spare any exaction from their subjects. That is how the historic core of Romania – Moldavia and Walachia – were ruled for centuries. No ruthless empire would tax its subjects to the point of exhaustion in any one year, but the Phanariots often did, for they had to recover their investment, accumulate more for the next auction, and keep themselves well-supplied in the meantime. Hence it was the lot of the Romanians to suffer one of the worst forms of governance ever devised, as remote in feeling from the subject culture as that of any empire, but without the moderating foresight that any empire must have – until next year's harvest tax at least.

To this observer at least, the Phanariot inheritance was manifest in the career of the Ceausescus, who did not merely oppress their subjects as other Communist rulers did and much more, but also exacted economic sacrifice to a unique degree. While the other regimes borrowed more and more from complaisant Western banks to calm their populations with a standard of living in excess of their feeble productivity, the Ceausescus only borrowed to finance their own Pharaonic schemes, then to repay the debts by driving their subjects to the edge of starvation. In the 1980s, while Czechs, East Germans, and Hungarians all ate more than they produced, Romanian food was exported in very large amounts; while all the others evaded even the energy crisis of 1973, throughout the 1980s no central heating was allowed in Romania in the bitter winter cold, nor enough light to read by comfortably. Only the Phanariots would confiscate even the seed grain at tax time, and only the Ceausescus would willfully impose the meanest level of war-rationing in peacetime, and then order more food exports still, leaving even those meager rations unfulfilled.

Unfortunately, the sinister Phanariot tradition has outlasted the Ceausescus, as it outlasted almost a century of full independence and partial democracy before communism under the enlightened Hohenzollern-Sigmaringen kings, of which the last—the perfectly decent and notably courageous King Michael—was driven from the throne at the end of 1947. (Still very much alive and well in Switzerland, he could yet bridge the constitutional gap as Spain's Juan Carlos did.)

Most harmfully, the Phanariot tradition still persists in the peasant and ex-peasant population at large, whose moral standards are no better or worse than that of any other such population, but which is too expectant of gross misrule to insist on better governance. And it persists most clearly in the present "National Salvation" regime, whose leaders have gone to the extreme—totally unimaginable anywhere else in ex-Communist lands—of courting renewed Soviet influence, for want of a Sultan to sanction their rule. Their politics are simple: an alliance of leading ex-Communist potentates determined to keep their villas, maids, and chauffered cars, with middling and lower ex-Communist officials equally determined to keep their apartments and pettier positions. Very few of them, all quite old, perhaps still believe in Communist ideology; most never did. Some see advantage in simulating democratic practices, but none of the leaders has so far manifested any visible desire for a genuinely democratic legality; all seem determined to rule subjects, not govern citizens.

Nestor Ratesh has given us a precious, uniquely penetrating account of the upheavals that preceded and followed the violent deaths of the Ceausescus. Readers will also find in his pages a most insightful assessment of the former regime in its progressive degeneration. But the author's most remarkable achievement for this reader at least is investigative: what follows is the first convincing depiction of Romania's revolution, entangled as it was by a conspiracy that still continues. Scholars will be grateful for the new evidence he has uncovered. The rest of us may be grateful that a work of such documentary importance is also so remarkably interesting for the nonspecialist reader, with none of the drama or most dramatic events slighted by the author's quest for accuracy amidst much deliberate deception and more confusion.

Edward Luttwak
The Arleigh Burke Chair in Strategy
The Center for Strategic and International Studies

June 1991

About the Author

Nestor Ratesh is the former head of Radio Free Europe's Romanian Broadcasting Department and currently its Washington senior correspondent. A native of Romania and a graduate of the Philosophy School of Bucharest University, Mr. Ratesh began his journalistic career as an editor of the Romanian News Agency. He emigrated to the United States in 1973 and became Radio Free Europe's Washington correspondent, broadcasting in Romanian, shortly afterward.

Since the violent uprising that toppled Nicolae Ceausescu's Communist dictatorship in December 1989, Mr. Ratesh interviewed many of the main players on the Romanian postrevolutionary scene, including President Ion Iliescu, former King Michael, opposition presidential candidates Radu Campeanu and Ion Ratiu, and ideologue and *éminence grise* of the National Salvation Front in the immediate aftermath of the revolution Silviu Brucan.

Previous works by Nestor Ratesh include essays and studies on Romania and U.S.-Romanian relations published by Praeger Publishers for the Center for Strategic and International Studies, by Freedom House, and by the American-Romanian Academy of Arts and Sciences.

Acknowledgments

My heartfelt thanks go first and foremost to the many friends and acquaintances in Bucharest and Timisoara who, by their testimony, thoughts, writings, and guidance, made this book possible. I am grateful to all who helped me bring this project to fruition, especially to my family and close friends, who encouraged me and stoically endured my peculiar behavior when I was afflicted by the "fever of creation." I owe thanks to Ambassador Patricia Lynch and others in Radio Free Europe's management who assisted me in more ways than one.

I am particularly indebted to Professor Virgil Nemoianu and to Paul Shapiro, both of whom reviewed the manuscript and made much-appreciated observations, to Michael Shafir, who was of great help in different stages of this endeavor, and to Victor Eskenasy, who offered his precious collection of videotapes and documents for my use. Many thanks are due to Carmen Pompey, Ioana Angelescu, and Dan Stancu for their assistance with my research. Last but not least, special gratitude goes to Veronika Capon, whose computer expertise guided me through the baffling maze of keys, modes, and attributes.

I hope each feels a measure of the satisfaction I feel in seeing this project completed.

Preface

It was a hazy day in late April 1990 when I set foot on Romanian soil for the first time in more than 17 years. Exactly four months had passed since the Christmas Day trial and execution of the former dictator Nicolae Ceausescu and his wife Elena—four short months in which the tremendous enthusiasm and exuberant optimism born with the revolution had turned, for many Romanians, into dark suspicions of plots and conspiracies that had hijacked the anti-Communist uprising.

Thousands of antigovernment demonstrators were filling University Square in the center of Bucharest in what was proclaimed a "zone free of neocommunism." Smaller solidarity rallies were taking place in other cities. The political arena was filled with the turbulence of Romania's first post-Communist, multiparty electoral campaign. Tempers were high, objectivity low, rumors and speculations abundant. Investigative exploits in such an environment are always hazardous, even more so those that touch on raw nerves and open wounds. My attempts to find out as much of the truth about the Romanian Revolution as the circumstances permitted were not always greeted with great enthusiasm. Nevertheless, they achieved a satisfactory success and formed the point of departure for this book. Careful screening of the Romanian and international press, on- and off-the-record interviews with many of the major players during and after the revolution both within Romania and abroad, and thorough analysis and comparisons of sources and interpretations have subsequently filled many gaps, dismissed some popular misconceptions, or simply proved the overwhelming difficulty of uncovering the truth with any certainty. Many of the initial perceptions have changed; question marks have replaced certainties; what seemed clear has turned foggy, and what was foggy has turned impenetrable.

This book, therefore, has no claim to definitive conclusions. It records, describes, comments, analyzes, scrutinizes, and labors to understand and make understood the exceedingly complex, tortuous, often baffling phenomenon that is called, sometimes reluctantly, the Romanian Revolution. The intent here is to stay squarely within the realm of known facts and serious, objective interpretation and to refrain from tempting speculation or plausible fancying, while exploring different versions, scenarios, and theories of the events of December 1989. The aftermath of the uprising was painful, with some clear attempts at restoration. There are those who think the revolution was stolen, confiscated, or hijacked. Others deem it unfinished. Still others doubt it was a spontaneous, popular revolt. All may have a point, although the final verdict belongs to history.

I call it simply the Entangled Revolution. It may yet be disentangled. Or it may repeat itself.

Washington, D.C.
June 1, 1991

Summary

This volume offers a full documentary account of the December 1989 revolution that toppled the Communist dictatorship of Nicolae Ceausescu in Romania. Based on the author's personal investigation and interviews, extensive screening of the Romanian and international press, and critical examination of sources and interpretations, it analyzes a complex, often puzzling series of events.

The author explores the economic, social, and human disaster that led to the uprising and then chronicles the seven days of the revolution from its inception in the Western city of Timisoara to its climax in Bucharest on December 22, 1989, when the dictator fled the city. The bloody and confused aftermath is examined from different angles, with surprising details and telling portraits of the main players, some of whom the author knows personally.

This volume scrutinizes the revelations, hints, and rumors of conspiracies that reportedly either caused the revolution – or hijacked it. Evidence available so far points toward a genuinely spontaneous popular uprising during which large segments of the army and secret police slowly realized that the fall of the regime was imminent. They first blinked, then searched for ways to save themselves – forcing Ceausescu to flee and bringing into power both new and old politicians who represented change to the masses but maintained relative stability in the power structure. The paradox that an essentially anti-Communist revolution would produce a regime controlled by former Communists has dominated most of the developments since then. The book concludes by examining the ensuing months of dislocation and commotion. Clearly the December revolution remains unfulfilled, "entangled in a myriad of contradictions, obstacles, intrigues, lies, rivalries, ineptitude, and plain wrongdoing."

Romania:
The Entangled
Revolution

1

The Foreseeable Revolution
That Nobody Foresaw

In the historic change that consumed the Communist regimes of Eastern Europe, Romania experienced the only violent uprising. It was bound to happen. By the end of 1989, Poland, Hungary, Czechoslovakia, East Germany, and even Bulgaria had been rapidly moving away from communism. The Soviet Union itself was in turmoil. The lone exception, aside from isolated Albania, was Romania. The Romanian dictator Nicolae Ceausescu had openly opposed any movement toward reform, casting himself with fierce determination in the role of last defender of communism.

Last Defender, Worst Offender

The last defender was the worst offender. Nowhere in Europe had the failure of communism been more stunning, the economic, social, and human disaster more desperate, the anguish of the people more heartbreaking. Every reason for a popular revolt was there: a huge accumulation of combustibles awaiting a spark. Nonetheless, although everybody conceded that Romania could not remain Eastern Europe's odd man out, no one to my knowledge actually predicted a revolution. There were some scenarios of change, from cos-

1

metic reforms to a palace coup. None included, however, a role for the Romanian people themselves.

From the start, most Western analysts had been none too deft in unraveling the true reality of Romania, beginning with the true nature of the Ceausescu regime. Over the years, they and the public alike had a hard time making the difficult spins to conform their thinking to the changing data on Romanian domestic and foreign policies. Back in the late 1960s, euphoria had conquered most minds. Romania was seen as the maverick nation of Eastern Europe, stirring trouble for the Soviet Union. Because it showed independence in foreign policy, it was viewed as moving away from the Soviet model of communism as well. To some Western analysts, nationalism equaled not only anti-Sovietism but also anticommunism. Many Romanians were making the same judgment at the time. But then, in the early 1970s, the regime reversed course domestically.

In 1973, when I left Romania to emigrate to the United States, the high hopes of the Romanian intelligentsia for a more liberal kind of socialism, with independence from the Soviet Union and closeness to the West, had already begun to crumble. It was becoming obvious that Nicolae Ceausescu had used the liberal pretense and the opening to the West as a means to consolidate his power and acquire absolute control over the party and state apparatus. The repulsive features of a peculiar cult of personality made their appearance on the Romanian scene. From the inside, ominous signs of the disaster to come could be seen by the sharp eyes of some skeptical Romanians. From the outside, however, such omens were either invisible or ignored. They would be ignored for many years, even when clear and shocking.

Quite shocking they became from the beginning of the 1980s. The erratic nature of the decision-making process, the taste for grand economic designs, and the delirious adulation of the leader and of his often irrational ideas brought calamity to the country and resulted in a monstrous society in which submission and fear replaced pride and incentives while lies and distortion posed as truth and trust. The shortages, the indignities, and the oppression kept piling up with no apparent end in sight. The rampant whims of the leader became absolute, crushing a people that seemed able to absorb obediently virtually any blow. Over the years, one question was asked more often in the West than any other: Where is the breaking point? Experts and common people alike wanted to know, how much more affliction will the Romanian people endure before they rise in anger and free themselves?

There was no good answer. In many instances it looked as if the limit of endurance had been reached, but it soon seemed that there was no limit. Many experts gave up on their attempts at guessing the reaction of the Romanians. Instead, they concentrated scholarly efforts on finding feeble explanations for the apparent inaction and passivity of the Romanian people in the nation's history and social psychology or in the harsh reality of daily existence.

Some intellectual endeavor was devoted to finding a formula that described the peculiarity of the Ceausescu regime in the 1970s and 1980s. For some, it was a primitive Stalinism. Others added a touch of Byzantine tradition to the classical communist totalitarianism, and still others spoke of an ersatz society, a pseudo-everything, including pseudo-neo-Stalinism.[1] There might have been a bit of all these ingredients, although in the end it looked in many respects like pure madness. There are certain things, including some basic options of the Romanian leadership, that can be convincingly explained in no terms other than the irrational.

Irrational Choices

With unbelievable tenacity, Nicolae Ceausescu and his clique conceived and executed an economic policy meant to industrialize Romania in a short time, with no regard whatsoever either for the real needs and interests of the country or for the human toll. The so-called accumulation rate (the percentage of the national income reinvested in the economy) was invariably kept at an excessively high level of about 30 percent to maintain a high rate of economic growth. Economic priorities and goals had been set arbitrarily, based mostly on the personal inclinations and preferences of the leader and his wife. The dictator's Stalinist fixation with heavy industry as a priority target led him to develop a colossal steel and metallurgical industry at any price. His wife's scientific pretense as a chemist called for a vast petrochemical industry. These industries became the pillars of the Romanian economy. Both turned out to be costly and unreasonable options.[2]

The basic economic flaw in these options was their complete disregard of Romania's lack of raw materials and energy resources. Although rich in natural resources, Romania has few raw materials for those particular industries that were Ceausescu's priorities. It was known for its oil reserves before and during World War II, but they did not amount to much in terms of modern consumption and processing needs. Consequently, all or most raw materials were imported, as was a large percentage of the energy used. In 1988, for example, imports of iron ore, which had increased almost 20 times since 1960 and more than 3.6 times since 1980, made up 86 percent of consumption; imports of apatite concentrates (the main raw material for fertilizers), which had grown 12 times since 1980, made up 100 percent of consumption, and imports of crude oil amounted to 67.1 percent of consumption.[3]

The paradox was that these industries virtually based on imported raw materials and energy could hardly sell their products on the world market. In 1988 (the year for which data are more or less complete), only 10.2 percent of the entire steel output was high-quality alloyed steel with a chance of being sold on the saturated world market. As a whole, heavy industry was not able to earn enough foreign currency even to cover the cost of the imported raw materials and energy it used. To compensate for this deficit, the regime constantly increased exports of food and consumer goods.

The priority industries were also energy-intensive industries at a time of scarce and expensive resources. Although they used more than half of all energy resources, their actual output amounted to only 18.9 percent of the entire industrial production. The case of the Slatina aluminum factory is often cited as a stunning illustration of this aberration. In 1989, the electrical consumption of this factory alone equaled the household consumption of the entire population of Romania.[4]

From Food Basket to Basket Case

While investing heavily in these priority targets and in megalomaniacal construction projects, the regime neglected other industries for which there was an adequate supply of domestic raw materials, primarily the food-processing and consumer goods factories. A tragic casualty of the regime's industrial policy was agriculture. Once "the food basket of Europe," Romania became a basket case – one, however, that pretended to be highly prosperous and found therefore no philanthropists. Fantastic exaggeration was exercised in reporting supercrops, as in the case of the 1989 grain harvest, which was pronounced by Ceausescu to have reached 60,000,000 tons but which turned out in reality to be less than 17,000,000 tons.

The obsessive industrialization had two devastating effects on agriculture: first, it deprived farm production of indispensable investments in machinery, irrigation, land conservation, and fertilizers; and second, it depopulated the countryside. The second result reached dramatic proportions, leaving the farm work largely to women and elderly people. Moreover, at a time when other Communist countries were easing land ownership laws and state controls over farm production, Ceausescu reintroduced compulsory deliveries to the state in 1983 and three years later decreed that all land was national property offered in temporary usage only to state and collective farms or individual farmers. State interference and plunder became totally unrestrained, killing any remaining incentives for better work or larger yields.

The outcome was desperately felt during the dictatorship; it is known now in precise figures. Farm productivity was one of the lowest in Europe. In 1989, corn yield per acre in Romania was only a fraction of what it was in other European countries, including Communist ones: 33 percent of Italy's or West Germany's yield, 45 percent of Hungary's, and 47 percent of Czechoslovakia's. Romania fared better in wheat production: less than 50 percent of West Germany's yield per acre, 55 percent of France's, 64 percent of Czechoslovakia's, and 70 percent of East Germany's. Milk production was much lower than in most European countries. Processed food was down substantially since 1980. In 1988, the Romanian food-processing industry's per capita output was as follows: meat – 37.2 kilograms (82.01 lb.); cheese – 3.2 kilograms (7.05 lb.); butter (with 30 percent margarine) – 1.7 kilograms (3.75 lb.); and oil – 14.2 kilograms (31.31 lb.).[5]

Even these meager resources could have provided a poor but passable diet for the people, had it not been for the frantic export of food for hard currency or energy. Ceausescu's decision to repay Romania's $12 billion foreign debt in a few years meant that everything that could be sold abroad for hard currency, raw materials, or energy was exported. Food products and consumer goods were among the easiest to sell. Although there is still no reliable data on how much was actually exported, there is ample evidence of unbearable shortages of basic food staples, most of them rationed, and of malnutrition, especially among children. In 1982 the regime, adding insult to injury, accused large segments of the population of overeating and consequently created a Rational Nourishment Commission to watch over the implementation of a Program of Scientific Nourishment. Hunting for food became the main concern of most people in the country, equal perhaps only to the anguish of cold in the winter.

With almost all domestically produced or imported energy gulped down by heavy industry, private consumption was reduced to a trickle. It was decreed that room temperature for common people could not exceed 50 degrees in winter. All that was permitted for lighting a room was one 40-watt bulb. In 1988, for example, only 5.4 percent of the electricity consumed in the country went to the people for household use. That percentage meant 530 watts per hour per person per day, on average.[6]

The Ethiopia of Europe

The ruling couple's grandiose delusions led to their attempt, through what was probably the world's most outrageous pronatalist policy, to increase substantially the population of Romania. At the 1984 Party Congress, Ceausescu set the goal of increasing the population of Romania from about 23 million to 30 million by the year 2000. In addition to banning the sale of contraceptives and almost all legal abortions, the regime introduced monthly compulsory gynecological examinations of all working women of childbearing age at their workplaces to determine when a woman became pregnant and to force her to carry the pregnancy to term. The result was not so much a rise in the birthrate (in 1989, the rate was a low 15.9 percent) as a tragic increase in the maternal mortality rate, from 86 deaths per 100,000 live births in 1966 to 150 in 1984, with 86 percent of them attributed to illegally performed abortions.[7]

All these harsh measures, which involved not only an unimaginable invasion of privacy but also severe punishment for any disobedience or violation, were taken at a time when common people simply could not feed their children or house them properly. Many children died in the hospital soon after they were born for lack of proper care, heat, and medicine. In 1989, the infant mortality rate was a very high

27 out of 1,000 children born alive, two or three times higher than that in other European nations or the United States.[8] Many other children were abandoned in overcrowded and abject orphanages – "warehouses for children," as the *Washington Post* called them. In a report from Romania, Mary Battiata of the *Washington Post* quoted Romanian and foreign sources that estimated the number of children housed in these orphanages at between 15,000 and 40,000. The conditions in such facilities were described by a French doctor as "something between Auschwitz and Kampuchea."[9]

The quality of life deteriorated during the 1980s to a startling extent. At the end of the decade, Romania ranked at or close to the bottom among the countries of Europe on virtually all indicators: health, housing conditions, clean air, access to radio and television, services, education, transportation, and so on. It was called "the Ethiopia of Europe."

The people's burden was greatly increased by having to hail the country's tormentor as its savior. Romanians lived a nightmare that they were told to call "the Golden Era." The one man largely responsible for the nation's misfortune was designated the "genius of the Carpathians," while his wife, who never attended any school beyond the fourth grade, became the "great scientist of world renown." These big lies were accompanied constantly by a myriad of smaller ones in a chorus of simulated collective madness. In Ted Koppel's apt metaphor, Ceausescu's Romania was "a madhouse in which the lunatics were running the asylum and the inmates were punished for their sanity."[10]

Punished they certainly were, as soon as they refused to play the game according to the "lunatics'" script. Not many took that risk, however. In fact, much of the population learned to play the game and, overwhelmed with fear, refrained from expressing their sanity and open protest against the regime. Hoping to survive the nightmare, the majority pretended the galoshes were actually a pair of cars. They were threatened; they were bribed; they were psychologically broken by a regime that fully applied

George Orwell's *1984* scenario with a minimum of updating. The extent of corruption and soul-selling in exchange for a slightly better chance of survival in the battle with hunger and frost is reflected in the cooperation many Romanians even gave their oppressors, mostly as informers of the pervasive security police (*Securitate*, in Romanian). It is said that one in every four or even three Romanians was an informer, an estimate that was never documented, although few have challenged it.

Isolated Resistance

The extensive chain of collaborators and the great number of people frightened into accommodation created a climate of submission that prevented the many accumulated combustibles from catching fire. That is not to say that Romanians did nothing but dance to the wacky tune of the leader. There were dissidents among the intellectuals and both hidden and open acts of resistance, including large strikes and violent unrest.

The largest act of opposition was the 1977 miners' strike of the Jiu Valley. During the month of August, 30,000 miners abandoned their work, demanding improvement in pay and standard of living. They would talk to no official but Ceausescu himself. When the dictator got there, the miners kept him captive until he promised to satisfy all their demands. As soon as he returned to Bucharest, however, Ceausescu unleashed a wave of terror upon the Jiu Valley. Most miners were forcibly moved to other regions of the country and reportedly replaced by other miners, *Securitate* troops, or collaborators, as well as young, inexperienced workers. Several leaders of the strike were killed in unexplained accidents. The international community learned about that serious challenge to the regime after it was over. Fragmentary information reached the West too late and through channels that were thought at the time to be insufficiently reliable. Even Radio Free Europe (RFE) was reluctant to broadcast the reports before confirmation by solid and credible sources.

It was different when the workers of Brasov, a beautiful city set in the Carpathian Mountains 150 miles north of Bucharest, took to the streets on November 15, 1987. The international press, including the Western radio stations, picked up the news and promptly spread it around the world. This time it was not just a strike centered on economic demands but a violent outburst with strong political overtones. It started at the large truck factory on the outskirts of Brasov, where negotiations between the workers and management on different economic demands had broken down earlier. Because November 15 was election day, the people were required to go to the voting centers and endorse the official candidates for "elective" positions. Instead, several hundred workers from the truck factory formed a column and marched toward the center of the city. By the time they got there, the crowd had swollen to 15,000. Chanting "Down with the dictator" and "Down with communism," the demonstrators stormed the party headquarters and set fire to Ceausescu's books and portraits and to posters and signs hailing the Communist Party.

At first the security forces for unknown reasons did not intervene. Later, however, special troops were brought in to quell the riots. Hundreds of people were apprehended, beaten, and tortured. Some of the leaders of the demonstrators disappeared; others were tried in December 1987 as "hoodlums" and given prison sentences of six months to three years. They were freed, however, and sent into interior exile to different towns far from Brasov. (Two and half years later, this same city was the scene of an act of epic self-sacrifice, when Liviu Babes set himself on fire on a ski slope on March 2, 1989, to protest the terror unleashed by the regime in the aftermath of the 1987 unrest. The act was widely reported by the international press at the time, although the name of the hero became known only later.)

In his first statement as a dissident, passed on to the United Press International (UPI) and British Broadcasting Corporation (BBC) correspondents in Bucharest, longtime

Marxist theoretician Silviu Brucan termed the Brasov riots "a turning point in the political history of Romania as a socialist state." He added: "A period of crisis has opened up in the relations between the Romanian Communist Party and the working class which until now has ensured the political stability of the regime." According to Brucan, the unrest signaled that "the cup of anger has spilled over and that the working class no longer accepts being treated as an obedient servant."

One year later, Brucan reportedly wrote the famous "Letter of Six," the most prominent public dissent within the party, gathering the signatures of several former leading figures of the Romanian Communist Party, including two former first secretaries. The sharply critical letter reached RFE in late February 1989, but with a clear specification from its signers that it not be broadcast before being carried first by other Western news organizations. (Apparently these old Communists were reluctant to be seen as airing their protest through an established anti-Communist medium.) During the early morning of March 11, 1989, the BBC broadcast excerpts of the letter. That same day RFE carried in its Romanian broadcast the full text of the letter, accompanied by the first analysis of the document. This open letter addressed to Ceausescu, which created a political platform for potential opposition within the party, stirred much interest abroad but did not have the expected impact in Romania, especially where it mattered most — that is, in the party apparatus.[11] It did, however, encourage more dissent and opposition, as reflected in the frequency and number of protest letters and statements that filtered abroad following its broadcast.

Some of the most significant acts of individual and group defiance of the Ceausescu dictatorship preceded the "Letter of Six" and were anti-Communist in nature. We have already mentioned the Jiu Valley strikes and the Brasov riots. In March 1979, a free trade union movement was formed with a membership of more than 2,000 people in different parts of the country. Its program included demands for rights unheard of in a Communist regime. The authorities hurriedly moved to stifle the new union by launching a savage hunt for its leaders. Some of them simply disappeared; others were jailed or forced to emigrate. Although it existed only two weeks, the Free Trade Union of the Working People of Romania (known in Romania by its acronym SLOMR) left a major imprint on the history of Romanian resistance to communism.

Intellectual dissent took longer to develop in Romania than in other Communist countries. It was in 1977, as a reverberation of the Charter '77 movement in Czechoslovakia, that the Goma group became the first meaningful political dissidence among the Romanian intelligentsia. Although few prominent intellectuals adhered to this movement, it left a long shadow that would be felt for many years. Writer Paul Goma already had a history of conflict with the Communist authorities when he wrote his open letter of solidarity with Charter '77: he had been detained twice and spent two years in prison in the 1950s, followed by five years of obligatory residence in a remote area. Between January and April 1977, Goma wrote several letters and appeals, some of them cosigned by as many as 200 people. He was arrested on April 1 and allowed to leave the country shortly afterward. From his exile in Paris, Goma never relented in his determined opposition to the Romanian Communist regime. Most of his group sought and received emigration visas (many of them were, in fact, a kind of Romanian refusenik). It was a common practice of the regime to give in sooner or later to pressures from the West and allow opponents to emigrate, faking compliance with the Helsinki agreements while at the same time neutralizing internal opposition by exporting it to the West. It happened in other prominent cases of dissent as well, among them historian Vlad Georgescu, poet Dorin Tudoran, and mathematician Mihai Botez, whose critical writings and acts of defiance left a lasting imprint on the Romanian intellectual community.

One kind of dissent that showed remarkable resilience even in the face of brutal repression or expatriation was the religious one. There were few known cases of opposition to the Ceausescu regime within the dominant Orthodox Church, but one stands out as quite remarkable. It is the case of Father Gheorghe Calciu Dumitreasa, whose strong anti-Communist sermons brought him years of imprisonment in the 1980s on top of other long years in jail during the 1950s and 1960s (a total of 21 years in Communist prisons). A more numerous and resolute challenge for the regime were the Protestant and Neoprotestant (Evangelical) denominations. Some of them were not even recognized by the government and found themselves in constant conflict with the authorities. Many of the leaders and clergymen of the Evangelical churches, as well as some of the believers, chose – or were forced – to emigrate.[12] The bulk of their membership and leadership stayed, however; their religious devotion, assertiveness, and foreign connections were a serious problem for the regime.

In the late 1980s, emigration ceased to be an option for most opponents of the dictatorship. The most impressive, active, and incisive critic of the regime during this period was Doina Cornea, the brave French teacher of Cluj. She strongly denounced the economic, human, and moral disaster in inspiring letters and statements smuggled out of Romania in different, often ingenious, ways.[13] Most of them were sent to RFE, which promptly broadcast them. She was harshly persecuted, closely watched, threatened, insulted, and beaten; but she never yielded. Doina Cornea was perhaps the best-known Romanian dissident internationally during the last convulsions of the Ceausescu tyranny and largely contributed to the international outcry against the dictator's insane plan of "systematization" of the countryside by the destruction of villages and the forced transfer of farmers into apartment buildings.

Noteworthy and of special impact both inside and outside Romania were poet Mircea Dinescu's writings and interviews, poet Dan Desliu's poignant letter of protest, Ana Blandiana's touching and unmasking poetry, Dan Petrescu and Gabriel Andreescu's lucid analyses, Radu Filipescu's mailbox leaflets (for which he was jailed), writer Aurel Dragos Munteanu's letters deploring the corruption of religion, and the courageous stand taken by other prominent intellectuals in publicly expressing their solidarity with Dinescu. Finally, the dissidence of former diplomat Dumitru Mazilu and his UN-sponsored report on the human rights of Romania's young generation (in fact, a document of a wider embrace) acquired considerable domestic and international resonance.

The Deadly Mix of Fear and Manipulation

It is impossible to know what practical effect, if any, this line of action may have had on the populace at large and on the regime itself. It is apparent that, although greatly admired, these people failed to transcend their isolation and to translate their daring acts into any significant movement. Except for the Jiu Valley and Brasov unrest and a few less-publicized occasional strikes or short-lived disturbances, no consequential event that attracted masses of people is known before the December uprising itself. The large reformist or opposition movements that guided change in other East and Central European nations were nonexistent in Romania, a fact that explains the amorphous and leaderless nature of the revolt.

The great debate over why Romania presented such a different political landscape continues. It will take some time before the answers, some of them painful, are sorted out. There are, however, a few noncontroversial, particular circumstances that may shed light on this knotty issue. One is, of course, the pervasive *Securitate* and its ability to control the entire population with insidious intrusions or with heavy-handed, violent, and even bloody repression. Also, the Mafia-like, tentacular power structure, in which the large family of the dictator and his wife occupied command positions, made any resistance from within the system impossible. The dire misery of everyday life, which enlisted virtually all energy, imagination, and inventiveness in the struggle for physical survival, served well the regime's purpose by leaving little time and vigor for political or social activism and even less for pursuits of the mind.

Another unique circumstance is the Romanian working class, which is much younger than the working class of other countries. It includes a large percentage of displaced peasants who have lost the solid values of the village without having yet assimilated urban behavior and outlook. This most vulnerable segment of the population was easily fooled, manipulated, and frightened. It was also hard for reform-minded people, especially intellectuals, to reach, even on those rare occasions when they tried. Romanian intellectuals are often accused of elitism and at least partially blamed for the lack of communication with the workers, which bordered on contempt. Whether the charge is true or not, the fact remains that there was no *Solidarność* or Civic Forum in Romania.

Instead, there was social and national division and hostility, carefully and viciously fostered. The nationalist diversion was highly successful in almost every direction it was pointed. The scourge of anti-Semitism was activated, a bit hindered by the smallness of the target (a Jewish population reduced by emigration to a mere 20,000 from a high of 400,000 at the end of the World War II) but quite effective in some intellectual circles. Anti-Hungarian hatred, assiduously exacerbated by the regime over many years, turned out to be quite potent. Finally, the anti-Russian sentiment was deftly put to work right from the beginning by Ceausescu, who built his reputation as a nationalist and independent-minded leader precisely on his perceived hostility toward Moscow.[14] It served him well both domestically and internationally. Ceausescu reaped every conceivable advantage from his much-publicized independence, which was of questionable benefit both to the West and to the Romanian people. For one thing, it allowed Ceausescu to turn Romania into his exclusive domain, oppress it at will, and make it a disaster area of the world, a country isolated and opaque to the rays of reform and change.

There is a certain responsibility that the West may bear and should recognize for letting itself be fooled by Ceausescu for so long for so little gain, and with so much harm. The West's meandering disposition towards Ceausescu is thought to have been an inhibiting factor for the potential opposition. This position is a legitimate and perhaps even justified point of view, although it often appears to be an attempt to "externalize" guilt, as analyst Michael Shafir would say, in the same class as the overused and misused Yalta agreement, and an excuse for inaction and submissiveness.[15]

The West finally cooled toward Ceausescu and in fact placed him in a kind of diplomatic quarantine in the second part of the 1980s. The United States, however, continued until 1988 to grant Ceausescu's Romania most favored nation (MFN) status, the highly visible symbol of what used to be a special relationship between the superpower of the West and a Warsaw Pact country (even then it was the Romanian dictator who preemptively "renounced" it).[16] By 1988 Romania was isolated both in the West and in the East, its appalling human rights record almost universally denounced. Ceausescu's response was to become the spoiler of the Helsinki process, which greatly accelerated during 1989. His role definitively made him an outcast in the European Community, which in turn significantly encouraged domestic opposition within Romania.

One thing is clear: the combustibles were there for years, incessantly piling up. Still, it seemed that nothing could set them ablaze – until that spark of December.

2

The Explosion

The spark flew in Timisoara. Why there? It may have been sheer chance – but more likely it was not.

The Timisoara Difference

Timisoara is the westernmost city of Romania and the capital of both the county of Timis and the historic region of Banat, which borders on Hungary and Yugoslavia. There is much history that nurtures local pride; among other things Timisoara has the distinction of being the first European city whose streets were lit by electricity (November 23, 1884).[1] A part of the Austro-Hungarian Empire until 1919, the city and its surrounding area maintained a Central European flavor even during the harsh years of communism. Fortunately, Ceausescu's reconstruction spell had not reached the beautiful cityscape of Timisoara, which remained generally whole and subtly provocative in its well-preserved architectural beauty. Much of the pain aroused by the sight of the destruction of Bucharest's old world charm and the wholesale neglect of its urban environment is alleviated when viewing stylish, clean, and neat Timisoara.

Moreover, unlike the hotly disputed region of Transylvania, Banat is known for a harmonious ethnic diversity with large numbers of Germans, Hungarians, Serbians, and other, smaller ethnic groups having lived alongside the Romanian majority for many generations. The ethnic diversity evolved into a religious diversity of great impact in a country with a dominant Eastern Orthodox Church. It created an environment of tolerance and openness that shaped a sense of togetherness and freedom. Pluralism had a real meaning here, although not in the political realm.

The proximity of the border allowed the people of Timisoara to remain in closer touch with the outside world. For one thing, they could easily watch Hungarian and Yugoslav television, which carried Western movies and shows and more informative newscasts, sometimes critical of the Ceausescu regime. Relatives and friends from the two neighboring countries frequently crossed the border with food and basic necessities unavailable in Romania. The large German minority maintained cultural and family ties with West Germany, where many Swabians and Saxons from Romania had emigrated in previous years.

Hardworking, exposed over many decades to beneficial influences and more advanced labor habits, and westernized in their mentality and behavior, the people of Banat were generally able to maintain a higher standard of living than the rest of the country and a specific, more civilized way of life. To Romanians and foreign visitors alike it was quite obvious what a world of difference there was between Banat and most other regions of Romania in many respects, not the least in the level of submission to tyranny.

A center of perennial discontent was the two higher education schools — the University of Timisoara and the Polytechnic Institute — with large campuses housing up to 20,000 students. Locals tell stories of numerous disturbances over the years, most of them related to local issues, but often with political overtones. Usually the outbreaks were quenched quietly. The local rulers carefully avoided publicity. Far away from the center of power, they had learned to allow for a certain amount of letting off steam to prevent serious outbursts of popular discontent.

Under these circumstances, a vigil at a small church was not seen as a major threat and was tolerated by the authorities for several days without serious interference. The vigil was to turn into the beginning of the Romanian Revolution.

Defending the Priest

The Reformed Church is located on a street corner in a square dominated by a beautiful shrine of the Virgin Mary, known by locals as Maria Square. From the outside, the church building does not look much different from an apartment building. In fact, there are several apartments in the four-storied building, including one that houses the congregation's minister and his family. The minister of the church was Laszlo Toekes.

The Reverend Laszlo Toekes's small church belongs to a denomination that has more than 700,000 followers, all of them ethnic Hungarians. It was one of the 14 denominations officially recognized by the atheistic Communist regime, and its activities were governed by numerous restrictions. In the case of the Reformed Church, however, the controls and the limitations were more severe than those applied to other religious groups because of its all-Hungarian membership. The bishops of the Reformed Church were generally submissive to the government, even obedient.

It was the Hungarian Reformed Church of Romania that was a few years ago at the center of one of the oddest charges brought by U.S. and international human rights organizations against the Romanian government. A large shipment of Bibles from the West was sent to the church, but it was never received by the addressee. It turned out that the Romanian authorities had simply recycled the Bibles into toilet paper. Strips of such paper with letters, words, and even sentences from the original Bibles still printed on them were presented as evidence to the public and congressional committees, stirring strong protests in

Western Europe and the United States. The issue was high-lighted at congressional hearings concerning renewal of MFN status for Romania. Nevertheless, the church hierar-chy is not known to have expressed any misgivings and is reported to have worked with the security police in silenc-ing critics within the church in this case. There were also reports of outspoken pastors and laymen of the Reformed Church being killed or molested in the past few years under circumstances that made critics believe that the *Securitate* was involved.[2]

Laszlo Toekes had been serving the Timisoara Re-formed Church since 1986. Son of Pastor Istvan Toekes, former professor at the Protestant Theological Institute of Cluj, he began his priesthood in Brasov, then was moved to Cluj. Alongside his father, the young priest involved him-self in opposition to state interference in the affairs of the Church and in defense of the rights of the Hungarian minor-ity. In reprimand, Istvan Toekes was dismissed from his influential position as vicar general of the Cluj diocese and as theology professor in 1984 and banned from the pulpit in early 1989. The son's career was also troubled. He too was excluded from the clergy in 1984 for "indiscipline." Two years later he was reinstated, first as chaplain and then as priest of the Timisoara Reformed Church.[3]

The Reverend Laszlo Toekes, whose sense of religious and civic duty put him on a collision course with both the ecclesiastic hierarchy of his denomination and the Commu-nist authorities, served as the immediate reason for the vigil that started around his church in mid-December 1989. His superiors accused him once more of "indiscipline," but this time a political charge was added—that "of entering in contact with political activists, foreign radio and TV sta-tions in order to denigrate and present in a tendentious way the realities of our country."[4] Most annoying for the regime was his strong criticism of Ceausescu's cherished plan for the so-called systematization of Romanian villages. On May 1, 1989, Laszlo Toekes was ordered transferred from Timisoara to a parish in the village of Mineu in the county of Salaj. Following the minister's refusal to comply with this order, his superiors asked the authorities (through a lawsuit) to evict him from the church building, which the authorities were quite eager to do, having incited the controversy in the first place to curb the pastor's political activities.

On Sunday, December 10, after the morning service, the minister told his congregation that the deadline for his eviction had been set for December 15. He asked the congregants to help him resist the eviction. A permanent vigil was set up at the entrance of the church building.[5] It sometimes attracted several hundred people, mostly Hungarian members of the congregation. They brought milk, bread, and firewood for their pastor and lit candles along the walls of the church. Slowly this defiance caught the imagination of many people in the city. Some would come to watch from a distance, and others would join the congregation. As the deadline for Laszlo Toekes's eviction drew closer, the crowd outside his church grew larger.

On December 15, the tension had reached a climax. As darkness fell upon Maria Square, the pastor made an appearance at a window of his apartment and addressed the crowd first in Hungarian and then in Romanian: "Dear Christians, we did nothing wrong. We preached the Gospel and now they want to evict us. Maybe they won't do it today, but surely they will do it tomorrow." The crowd replied: "Never, never! We won't desert you! We won't leave this place!"

By then the crowd had grown substantially. The several hundred Hungarian congregants were joined by a growing number of Romanian sympathizers who had heard about the pastor's plight from friends or from foreign radio broadcasts. Plainclothes policemen were sent to harass the people. Shortly after 7:00 P.M. they attempted to take into custody a man who was crying for help. That incident provoked the first known clash between the police and the demonstrators. More than 1,000 people were gathered around the church when the clash occurred. Hundreds and perhaps thousands of candles were lighting the square. The traffic had virtually stopped on the adjacent wide "Sixth of March" Boulevard. The streetcars were blocked in both directions in Maria Square. As the police became more aggressive, the number of clashes increased as well. At one point, Laszlo Toekes himself appeared again at his window to appeal for calm. The deadline had passed; the pastor was still in the church building.

Next day, Saturday the sixteenth, the mayor of Timisoara himself came to the church to persuade the people to go home. He appeared with Pastor Toekes at the apartment window, making an attempt to talk to the crowd, but the jeers drowned out his words. Only at the request of the pastor was he allowed to speak. The mayor said that the eviction order against the minister had been rescinded and the minister could remain with his congregation and in his apartment. The crowd applauded. Some of the people left happy, but most stayed behind. Something seemed wrong. When the minister asked them to leave, they noticed a stranger behind him. The minister appeared to be following orders.

The Last Day of Vigil, the First Day of Revolution

By late afternoon, the crowd had increased dramatically, and it was a different crowd. Many young people, high school and university students, joined the vigil. The language spoken by most demonstrators was not Hungarian as before, but Romanian. Traffic was stopped again. The demonstrators chanted "Freedom, freedom." A column was formed, beginning to move toward the Maria bridge over the Bega Canal toward the center of the city. According to eyewitness accounts, they wanted to reach the students' dorms. The mood and the slogans changed markedly. They chanted "Down with Ceausescu" and "Down with the dictator."

At this moment the vigil around the Reformed Church turned into an anti-Communist uprising. Maria Square remained a focal point of the movement, but the center of the city became the battlefield of the uprising. As the new column was leaving Maria Square, a bus full of militiamen arrived and separated the church congregants from the rest of the crowd. Shortly afterward, two fire engines suddenly arrived and began spraying the people guarding the entrance to the church. Surprised, people ran for cover. In the meantime, the militia blocked all access to Maria Square. The crowd fought the troops with pavement rocks and bottles. The column of demonstrators, several hundred strong, crossed the bridge and headed toward the students' dorms. On their way they destroyed posters and signs glorifying Ceausescu. New slogans were chanted: "Down with the Communist Party," "Down with the dictatorship," "It's now or never," and the prophetical "Today in Timisoara, tomorrow in the whole country." The old revolutionary and nationalistic song "Wake up, Romanian" was sung for the first time.

Taking the route back from the campus to the center of the city, the column merged with a group of demonstrators marching from a different direction. When the crowd reached the downtown area, it numbered 5,000 people. It was heading toward the county headquarters of the Communist Party, a large building on a wide, tree-lined boulevard, not far from the modern Continental Hotel. As they were approaching it, the demonstrators were met by two fire engines spraying water on them. The crowd attacked them head on; one fire engine managed to leave, the other was destroyed.

When the demonstrators reached the party headquarters just before 9:00 P.M., the lights were off in all offices, the guards gone, and the building deserted. Nobody was there to engage in a dialogue with the demonstrators. Enraged, the crowd broke windows and destroyed the Communist Party flag. Dozens of books by the dictator and his wife were taken from a nearby bookstore and set on fire in front of the party headquarters. Some demonstrators tried to enter the building, but the heavy door could not be opened.

Around 9:30 P.M., troops in the blue uniforms of the Interior Ministry arrived in the area. Armed with wooden sticks and tear gas, they attacked the demonstrators. The crowd resisted for a while, and then a new slogan was launched: "No violence." The first violent encounter between troops and demonstrators ended with a few injuries and several people arrested (and tortured behind the party building). The crowd split into two columns that went in different directions. Most of the demonstrators headed for the Opera Square, a large and beautiful mall flanked on one side by the opera house and on the other side by the Orthodox cathedral.

By evening, the uprising had spread rapidly around the city. Groups of people constantly formed in different neighborhoods. Marching the streets of a particular neighborhood, they called on the people to join them. Then they headed toward the center of the city. At one point during the evening, many of the demonstrators gathered in front of the Orthodox cathedral to ask the Metropolitan Nicolae of Banat to serve as a conduit to the local party leadership, with whom they wanted to open a dialogue. The Metropolitan was on a trip abroad, but they stayed there anyhow, believing they were safer in front of that historic monument. At midnight, the crowd was estimated at 10,000. Not far from there, just across the bridge, Maria Square was almost deserted. The troops had been in control there for several hours.

The first day of the Romanian Revolution came to a relatively quiet end. The people in front of the cathedral chanted slogans and sang songs. Crowds filled other squares as well. Clashes with the troops were reported in some parts of the city, with few injuries and no deaths. In no instance were firearms used on either side during that day.

The Day to Remember

During the night, a column of demonstrators left the cathedral for the northern boroughs of the city. They clashed with troops and then dispersed. Few people slept that night; there was much excitement all over the city. In Maria Square, however, the authorities got their prize: in the early hours of the morning, officers of the *Securitate* broke into the Reformed Church, beat the Reverend Laszlo Toekes, and took him in custody. At the time, this event passed almost unnoticed; the revolution was already under way. That Sunday, December 17, 1989, was to become the bloodiest day in the history of Timisoara – and the day that would mark the beginning of the end for Ceausescu's dictatorship.

Dawn found the city under virtual military occupation. During the night, troops and armored personnel carriers had been deployed all over the city. Units with flags and bands paraded the streets. Obviously, the army and security police were undertaking a show of force in an attempt to intimidate the population. Nevertheless, thousands of people found their way to the center of the city, gathering mainly in the spacious mall between the opera house and the cathedral.

Around noon, the crowd in Opera Square started to move toward the county headquarters of the Communist Party to request a dialogue with the authorities. The way, however, was blocked by several rows of troops, two water cannons, a fire engine, and two trucks. The crowd kept advancing. The troops retreated, letting the water cannons spray the demonstrators, but to no avail. The crowd took over the water cannons and the trucks. Someone cried "No violence." The soldiers fled, taking refuge on a side street. As soon as the crowd got to the front of the party headquarters, some people forced their way into the building by breaking the front door. Other demonstrators followed them. They found a Romanian flag in the main conference room and cut out the Communist coat of arms, leaving a hole in the middle. A young girl took it out on the balcony and waved it to the crowd gathered in front of the building. This seems to have been the first time that the holed flag became a symbol of the Romanian Revolution, patterned after the Hungarian precedent of 1956. Ceausescu's portraits were thrown out in the street. A fire was lit on the ground floor.

The demonstrators were in control of the building for less than 20 minutes. It was shortly after 2:00 P.M. when special units dressed in blue overalls and white helmets and armed with rifles with fixed bayonets attacked the crowd. Those inside the building left hurriedly and clashed with the troops. A pregnant woman was stabbed in the abdomen by one of the attackers. Many other demonstrators were hit. Some were arrested and savagely beaten on the spot. Finally, the crowd was dispersed. Armored cars blocked several streets and were stationed in many strategic parts of the city. One was seen chasing and crushing a pregnant woman holding a child in her arms. Another woman had the same fate. Several clashes were reported in the area. At least one tank was set on fire by the crowd. By 4:00 P.M., most of the demonstrators had managed to escape, retreating to Opera Square, which was already full of people. Dark was beginning to set in, but the balmy, spring-like day had yet to see the most tragic events for which it would be remembered in history.

Ceausescu: Shoot to Kill

As the demonstrators were returning from the Communist Party county headquarters to Opera Square in Timisoara, an emergency meeting of the ruling Political Executive Committee was hurriedly convened in Bucharest. Informing the committee about events in Timisoara, Ceausescu insisted on "the interference of circles from abroad, foreign espionage circles, beginning with Budapest. . . . It is also known," he added, "that both in the East and in the West everybody talks about the need to change things in Romania. Both those in the East and those in the West have set out to change and use everything [to this end]." He came back to the subject several times during the meeting. At one point, he said that "the East and the West had united in order to destroy socialism, because what they want is a humane, capitalist socialism."[6]

Raging with fury, both Nicolae and Elena Ceausescu took to task Minister of Defense Vasile Milea and Minister of the Interior Tudor Postelnicu for their inability to put down the uprising in Timisoara promptly, the main charge being that they did not arm their troops sent to fight the demonstrators with live ammunition. "Why?" asked the dictator angrily. "I told you to arm them all. Why did you send them unarmed? I discussed with you many times during the night, at 2:00, and at 3:00, and at 4:00 in the morning what you had to do. . . . What did your officers do, Milea? Why didn't they intervene immediately? Why didn't they shoot? . . . What kind of a Defense Minister are you? What kind of an Interior Minister are you, Postelnicu?" Elena Ceausescu jumped in: "The situation is very grave and unpleasant." "It is grave and you are to blame," concluded Nicolae Ceausescu, adding a little later, "I, as commander-in-chief, think you have betrayed the interests of the country, of the people, of socialism, and did not act responsibly."

This statement obviously was an extremely serious accusation with tragic consequences for the two ministers. Indeed, the dictator was ready to take the next step: "As of this moment, if the Political Executive Committee agrees, we dismiss the Minister of National Defense, the Minister of the Interior and the commander of the *Securitate* forces. As of this moment, I take over the command of the army. . . . I trust such men no more. We cannot go on like this. . . . They should have killed the hooligans, instead of being beaten by them. . . . You know what I should do? Put you in front of a firing squad! This is what you deserve, because what you have done means joining forces with the enemy." Nevertheless, the two ministers were saved (temporarily in the case of the defense minister, as things later turned out) by the suggestion of other committee members to give them one more chance to show their loyalty and toughness in Timisoara.[7]

In any case, Ceausescu ordered "to immediately, right now, arm the troops [with live ammunition] and have them carry out the order [to shoot]. . . . Therefore immediate measures must be taken to rapidly liquidate what is happening in Timisoara, bring the army in a state of alert, in a fighting state, both the units of the Interior Ministry and those of the Defense Ministry and wherever there is an attempt of [antigovernment] action, liquidate it radically, without a word."[8]

The Political Executive Committee of the Communist Party formally approved Ceausescu's decision. The two ministers and the commander of the security forces, General Iulian Vlad, promised to do their best to execute the decision. Everything seemed settled for the moment—but not for Ceausescu, who wanted a final confrontation that would expose any cracks or treason within the committee. According to an eyewitness, toward the end of the meeting, he suddenly jumped up, flung the papers in front of him, and in violent wrath shouted to those present: "Then elect yourselves another Secretary General!" As the dictator made his way toward the door, several of his subordinates ran after him. Falling to their knees, they begged him to stay, apologized, and made promises of good conduct. The women cried. The uproar came to an end when Elena Ceausescu spoke. "Leave Comrade Ceausescu alone for a moment," she said. "I will try to convince him not to resign." She certainly succeeded.[9]

There is little doubt that it was all staged. Just outside the meeting hall, dozens of security guards were ready to intervene at the first sign of trouble. Those inside knew it. Still, one cannot help speculating what would have happened had the members of the Political Executive Committee accepted Ceausescu's resignation. Of course, however, they were not the kind of people who would put the interests of the country before their own.

Bloody Sunday

While this farce was being played in the Central Committee building in Bucharest, two of the dictator's top aides were already on their way to Timisoara. One of them was Ion Coman, a member of the Political Executive Committee and secretary of the Central Committee in charge of the army and *Securitate*. During the meeting described previously, the dictator impatiently asked whether Coman had arrived in Timisoara and instructed his secretary to have him call as soon as he got there. When Coman arrived, he took command of all forces in Timisoara and implemented Ceausescu's order to open fire on the crowds.

Even prior to Coman's arrival some isolated shooting was reported.[10] Shortly after 5:00 P.M., however, heavy shooting was suddenly directed toward the crowd that had gathered in Liberty Square. The people there were taken by surprise. Few believed that the soldiers would shoot to kill. For some unexplained reason, the protestors thought that either the authorities would not dare to massacre the people or the army would not follow orders to shoot with live ammunition. On the ground, however, were the first casualties. Many demonstrators started to crawl for cover behind trees. Others were running toward the neighboring park. The bullets came from everywhere. Hell had broken loose all over the place. In the central square between the opera house and the cathedral, stores were devastated, looted, and set on fire. Witnesses say they saw bands of drunken men systematically destroying and looting the stores. Dubious-looking individuals were carrying large packages of goods, including cosmetics and furs, while many in the crowd shouted, "Brothers, don't destroy, don't steal!" The eyewitnesses are convinced that those looters were *Securitate* agents sent to stage such acts to create the pretext for repression.[11]

Repression was not long in coming. There were several thousand people in the square, many of them massed in front or on the steps of the locked cathedral. A substantial number of those who managed to flee the shooting in Liberty Square joined the crowd at the opera house and the cathedral. Occasionally the crowd would chant: "Freedom, freedom," "Down with Ceausescu," "No violence," or "We are the people." The song "Wake up, Romanian" was heard repeatedly. A few peaceful confrontations with the troops stationed in the square were reported at the beginning of the evening. Around 7:15 P.M., with no warning, the troops started to shoot in all directions. Several people on the steps of the Cathedral fell to the ground, wounded or dead. Others took refuge behind the church or fled to the neighboring parks and smaller streets. Heavy shooting was under way in other central locations: in Maria Square, on Republicii Boulevard, in the 700 Square, and at the Continental Hotel. The shooting came from different sources: soldiers in orderly formations, moving armored cars, and officers in plain clothes. It would appear that most of the shooting was directed in the air or to the ground, either in keeping with orders or by reluctant officers and soldiers, some of them seen crying.

There were clashes in the suburbs as well, some of the more serious occurring in the working-class neighborhoods. A major battle between troops and demonstrators took place on Calea Girocului, where about 2,000 demonstrators blocked the way of armored vehicles headed for the center of the city. The crowd captured the crews and took over the tanks, trying to disable the tanks as best they could.

It did not take long for the reinforcements to show up and attempt to recover the tanks and the crews. Just before 9:00 P.M., troops coming from both sides of the road approached the crowd. They were received with jeers and rocks. Some demonstrators tried to talk to the soldiers, telling them that they too were part of the people and should not shoot at their brothers and sisters.

Suddenly, two red rockets lighted the sky, the signal for the troops to open fire. They first shot in the air to try to scare the people into fleeing, but few did. The troops then opened fire directly into the crowd. Several people fell dead or injured. The crowd retreated; many fled in all directions. Large groups formed again at some distance and started to break windows and vandalize stores in a nearby shopping center in revenge. A large bonfire was lit in the middle of the road with books containing the dictator's speeches and his wife's "scientific" works. At about 11:00 P.M., new troops arrived from the center of the city. While the shooting – at people, toward balconies and apartment windows, and into the air – continued, the soldiers were also making great efforts to put the tanks in motion. In the early hours of the morning, the troops finally left the area.

At about the same time, an unusual summer-like storm with blinding lightning and deafening thunder descended on the city. The heavy downpour cleaned the streets somewhat. Many blood stains would stay on, however – for a day or two on the pavement, forever in the consciousness of the Romanian people.

Off to Iran

On Monday the eighteenth, Timisoara resembled an occupied city, with massive military forces deployed all over, mopping up operations under way in different neighborhoods, hospitals full of wounded people, and bodies of the dead stolen by the *Securitate* from the morgue and sometimes from their own homes and taken away for secret burials or incineration. A large number of people were detained, beaten, and tortured. All access roads to the city were blocked. All telephone connections with the rest of the country as well as all international lines had been cut. No mail service was available. A few relatively small demonstrations and clashes did take place at the Orthodox cathedral, in the downtown area parks, and in at least one working-class neighborhood. Uniformed troops flanked by plainclothes officers occasionally shot at the demonstrators. Armored personnel carriers were also used to attack groups of protesters. Following orders from Bucharest, local party officials organized rallies in factories, offices, and schools to condemn "the acts of vandalism perpetrated by hooligans." The regime seemed in control, but beneath the surface tensions were building to a point of no return.

In Bucharest, Ceausescu must have been satisfied and confident that the crisis had been overcome: He went ahead with his planned trip to Iran. The previous evening, he had summoned another meeting of the Political Executive Committee, the second that day. He directed his subordinates to inform all the counties that "we are in a state of war" and that all units of the Interior Ministry and of the *Securitate* were put on a state of alert throughout the entire country. At the same time, all international tourism was stopped. "No foreign tourist should come anymore because all have become espionage agents," Ceausescu stated. He appointed Elena Ceausescu (who, for a change, was not to accompany him on that trip) and Vice President Manea Manescu to "coordinate" party and government work.[12]

Nicolae Ceausescu boarded his special presidential plane at 9:30 A.M. on Monday, December 18 with the usual pompous protocol, but hardly in good spirits. It was a measure of his demented self-confidence that he embarked on a foreign trip in the midst of the most serious challenge ever to his rule, and to the Communist regime in general. A possible loss of prestige must have weighed heavily in his reluctance to postpone the trip. Moreover, such a last-minute postponement, just as the first news about the massacre in Timisoara had filtered to the outside world, would have been seen both abroad and within Romania as a confirmation of the seriousness of the situation. In retrospect, however, this visit, which was long on honors and short on tangible results, turned out to have been one of the most serious mistakes made by the dictator during his last week in power. Far from reassuring anybody about the domestic situation, it had the opposite effect, at least in Timisoara, which was rife with rumors that Ceausescu in fact had fled the country. One slogan heard in front of the cathedral on Monday afternoon was, "The rascal Oltean has fled to Teheran."[13] (Unconfirmed later reports have indeed mentioned the possibility that Ceausescu may have gone to Teheran to arrange his flight to Iran, if overthrown.)

In any case, by the time he came back from Iran, the situation in Timisoara had become untenable, with a general strike and huge demonstrations, the army fraternizing with the people, and all attempts to negotiate an end to the uprising totally unsuccessful. Moreover, the news of the Timisoara revolt had reached Romanians all over the country through foreign radio broadcasts. The uprising spread to other cities, such as Cluj, Arad, Brasov, Sibiu, and Tirgu Mures. Bucharest itself was very tense and on the verge of exploding.

Victory in Timisoara

While Ceausescu was in Teheran, a high-level delegation, headed by Prime Minister Constantin Dascalescu and Emil Bobu, reputedly the most powerful person in the Romanian Communist leadership next to the ruling couple, went to Timisoara. Other top officials, including members of the government and commanders of the army and security forces, were already there on different assignments related to the quenching of the uprising. They made every effort to try to stop the demonstrations either by intimidation, deception, and political maneuvering or by brutal force. None succeeded.

A general strike was in effect in the whole city on Tuesday, December 19. Several clashes occurred between workers and military forces in different parts of the city. Shots were fired, and eyewitness accounts reported casualties. By midnight, however, all shooting came to an end as if by magic. It was not resumed for two days and then under totally different circumstances.

On Wednesday, Timisoara was a different city. In the

morning, huge columns of people converged on the center of
the city. The army allowed them to pass without incident.
Around noon, the army was fraternizing with the people.
The tanks and armored personnel carriers were crowded by
clusters of demonstrators. The battle cry "The army is with
us!" had finally acquired real meaning.

A big crowd filled Opera Square. Another crowd occupied the large space in front of the Communist Party
county headquarters. Several of the bosses from Bucharest were there. Prime Minister Dascalescu and the local
party boss Balan made an appearance on the balcony in
an attempt to speak to the people. They were jeered and
booed. The demonstrators chanted: "Down with Ceausescu!
We want free elections! Democracy! Liberty! Where are our
dead?" In the meantime, from the opera house balcony
different speakers addressed the demonstrators. "We won't
leave! Today in Timisoara, tomorrow in the whole country!"
chanted the crowd. The first revolutionary committees were
formed.

Around 3:00 P.M., the prime minister asked to talk to
the representatives of the demonstrators. A delegation of
13 to 18 people (the eyewitness accounts differ on this) was
quickly put together and went up to the first-floor conference room of the party county headquarters, where Dascalescu and several other party and government top officials
were waiting for them. Nothing came out of those talks,
which dragged on for several hours. The prime minister
made some vague promises on minor issues but said that
major demands, such as resignation by Ceausescu and the
government, would have to await the president's return
from Iran, expected in late afternoon that same day. In fact,
Dascalescu was trying to gain time. The talks ended incon-
clusively just before 7:00 P.M. The prime minister boarded a
plane to return to Bucharest shortly afterward. The people
were in charge of the city. For all practical purposes, the
revolution was victorious in Timisoara. Would the rest of
the country follow? Did they know about it?

The News Spreads on Shortwave

That evening of December 20, Romanians around the country heard for the first time on their official radio and television about developments in Timisoara from Ceausescu himself. Most of them already knew much more than the dictator would dare to tell them.

The first news about the violent repression of the Timisoara demonstrations was broadcast to Romania by the BBC during the late afternoon of December 17, the day of the massacre, but its audience was relatively small. With the largest Romanian audience of all Western radio stations, RFE would follow suit that same evening.[14] It carried a short news item on its late evening newscast, quoting a Hungarian television report about clashes between supporters of the Protestant priest Laszlo Toekes and the militia. It said that several people were arrested but made no mention of any shooting or casualties. One hour later, again in the newscast and quoting Hungarian and Western media, RFE informed its Romanian listeners that the vigil at the Reformed Church had turned into an anti-Ceausescu demonstration. No other details were given. At that time the information was scant and uncertain, coming mostly from travelers who managed to cross the border from Romania into Hungary or Yugoslavia. Their stories seemed quite incredible at the time and were viewed with a good deal of skepticism. Because of the explosive nature of the news, it was treated with great caution. Nevertheless, RFE's Romanian broadcast, which usually goes off the air at 1:00 A.M., stayed on all night with a program of live uninterrupted music and news. Although there was little new information during that night, the sheer fact of an all-night broadcast gave listeners a sense of urgency and a hint that something of consequence was happening. Indeed, many Romanians would later testify to the great excitement of that night.

The reports became more abundant and more reliable early the next day, and RFE canceled its regular programs to go live with factual reports, reactions from all over the world, and some preliminary and very cautious comments. During the evening broadcast the first two eyewitnesses were interviewed over the telephone from Vienna, one of them crying as he described in vivid detail the bloody events. For the first time the slogan "Today in Timisoara, tomorrow in the whole country" was heard over RFE.

That same evening, Radio Bucharest, in its first hint but with no direct reference to Timisoara, warned the population about "a real offensive by reactionary, imperialist circles against socialism aiming at destabilizing the situation in the socialist countries, diminishing socialism and weakening its stand in Europe and worldwide." The official Romanian Radio peremptorily stated that it was "imperative to reject with great determination" such attempts. A clearer hint of the seriousness of the situation was given the next day by the party newspaper *Scinteia* in an unsigned commentary calling for "the consistent promotion of the rule of law" and for "the spirit and letter of the law to be applied in every field and in every circumstance."

By then, the whole world was aware of and horrified by the harsh repression in Timisoara. The U.S. government had condemned the use of force in Timisoara on December 18. A statement read by State Department spokeswoman Margaret Tutwiler stressed that because the Romanian government "does not have the support of the people, it is following a terribly mistaken course of using security forces to repress a serious manifestation of popular discontent." The British government issued a travel advisory to its citizens planning to visit Romania, while Deputy Foreign Minister William Waldegrave called on the Romanians "working for the state" to "put an end to this regime." West German Chancellor Kohl called the repression "abominable." The European Economic Community (EEC) froze the agreements negotiated with Romania. Condemnations came from both the Council of Europe and the North Atlantic Treaty Organization (NATO).

In East Berlin, the participants in the roundtable nego-
tiation for democracy called on the Romanian government
to end the repression. The Polish parliament passed a resolution protesting the violation of human rights in Romania.
The Hungarian parliament requested that the Romanian
government respect the commitments it undertook in international agreements regarding human rights. It instructed
the Hungarian government to protest the repression in
Timisoara at the United Nations. In Sofia, 1,000 Bulgari-
ans protested in front of the Romanian embassy, request-
ing, among other things, that Bulgaria cut all ties with the
Romanian government. Soviet Foreign Minister Eduard
Shevardnadze, asked about Timisoara while on a visit to
Brussels, expressed his "deep regret if indeed some loss of
life has occurred there." The Soviet minister was still reluctant to align his statements with those, more severe, of the
West and of some Eastern countries.

Ceausescu on the Offensive

Ceausescu was not impressed by the international outcry.
He came back from Iran in no mood to apologize or retreat.
Instead he went on the offensive with a televised speech in
which he dismissed the demonstrators in Timisoara as "a
gang of hooligans" manipulated by foreign agents and set
to destroy and loot shops and public buildings. The address
was broadcast on December 20, at night, a few hours after
the dictator's return from Iran. He said that the army was
compelled, in response to provocation, to defend itself but
made no mention of the shooting and deaths. Although he
accused "reactionary" and "imperialist" forces in general of
fomenting the turmoil, he placed the responsibility squarely at Budapest's door. Several times he repeated that foreign espionage services were to blame for the disturbances,
which were aimed at breaking up Romania. Ceausescu appealed to the Romanian people to prevent a recurrence of

the Timisoara events in other parts of the country, shrouding the whole crisis in terms of a battle to preserve Romania's independence and territorial integrity.

Still on the offensive, Ceausescu called for a mass meeting of support in Palace Square in Bucharest the next day. It is not known whose idea this rally was. It was probably Ceausescu's. In his self-confidence, he apparently believed that a rousing speech and enthusiastic cheers could help put an end to the crisis. Some have suggested that he may have been in the dark about the gravity of the situation, even though his televised address the night before betrayed concern and alarm. In any case, it turned out to be his fatal mistake.

The people in different factories and offices had been told about the rally the morning before. Then around 2:00 P.M. the meeting was canceled. A little later it was on again, and on it stayed. It is still unclear what caused the wavering. Ceausescu was not yet back in town, and somebody may have had afterthoughts. Next morning, as they had done many times before, thousands upon thousands of workers, closely watched by party organizers and security officers, gathered in preannounced places and were taken to Palace Square. The city was under virtual martial law, with troops patrolling the streets and guarding important buildings.

The Ceausescus appeared on the main balcony of the Central Committee building in the company of the other members of the party leadership. The people cheered, chanting as usual "Ceausescu-Romania, our esteem and pride." First, other speakers blasted the "hooligans" of Timisoara and praised the "wise leadership" of the Communist Party. Then Ceausescu himself took the floor.

Ceausescu began his speech by extending "warm revolutionary greetings and best wishes for success" (cheers, chants). As he was thanking the organizers of the rally, about a minute or so into the speech, a big commotion started suddenly, and high-pitched screams were heard in the background. Ceausescu's voice faded, and the TV and radio relay was interrupted. Patriotic songs were played instead. The broadcast from the square was resumed after about three minutes with Ceausescu in the middle of a sentence: "... strength and unity in defending the independence, integrity and sovereignty of Romania." The speaker was interrupted several times by applause, some unintelligible shouting, chants, and more commotion. He announced measures he said were adopted that morning by the Political Executive Committee regarding pay and pension increases and the introduction of a maternity allowance. He was obviously disturbed and could hardly continue the speech. After a couple of sentences about Timisoara, he abruptly stopped and left the balcony, hurriedly followed by the others.

The television viewers could sense that something unusual was occurring in the square but did not know for sure what had happened. Shortly before the broadcast was interrupted, from the back of the crowd chants of "Timisoara! Timisoara!" were heard. According to eyewitness accounts published in the Romanian press, a small group of young workers from the Turbomecanica factory had started the turbulence.[15] When they first heard about the rally, they decided to do something in the hope that other people would follow them. They took hold of a couple of flags and waited nervously through the speeches that preceded Ceausescu's. Shortly after the dictator began his speech, they started to wave the flags and shout "Timisoara! Timisoara!" "Down with Ceausescu!" "You killed our innocent children!" The people around them, surprised and terrified, quickly moved away from them. To avoid being caught, the protesters rushed forward through the crowd, continuing to chant their slogans. At about the same time, another lone protester by the name of Nica Leon started to shout anti-Ceausescu slogans. Afraid that the security forces would open fire, the crowd kept a distance from the courageous demonstrators. Many began to run, dropping the flags, portraits, and signs they were carrying.

The confusion grew rapidly, while Ceausescu, perplexed

by the sudden shifting of the mass of people in the square, interrupted his speech and looked helplessly to his wife, apparently not knowing what to do. The rear rows of people were disbanding. Hundreds, perhaps thousands were leaving the square, some running panic-stricken. Nobody was trying to stop them. After a few minutes, somebody appealed to the crowd over the loudspeakers: "Citizens, please go back to your previous places. Nothing happened." Ceausescu then resumed his speech, but the rally ended in pandemonium.[16]

Timisoara in Bucharest

The young workers managed to lose themselves in the fleeing crowd, disappointed that they were not followed by other people, convinced that they had failed in their attempt to stir trouble, and fearful that they would be hunted down by the *Securitate*. One of them went straight to the railroad station and took the train to Brasov. The others moved around, trying to avoid being caught. Their disappointment, however, turned out to be unfounded. In fact, even before the rally came to an end, bands of youngsters started to move, through alleys, courtyards and passages, toward University Square and the Intercontinental Hotel, one block behind the Central Committee building, where they formed several separate groups that later merged as their numbers increased to several hundred and then to several thousand. They cut out the Communist coat of arms from the flags, burned portraits of the ruling couple and posters with official slogans, and chanted "Down with the tyrant!" Security troops and militiamen showed up almost immediately and arrested or beat up some demonstrators on the fringes of the compact crowd.

For a couple of hours, in early afternoon, the demonstration was peaceful, the troops and the protesters facing each other in relative calm. Even some goodwill gestures from the demonstrators toward the troops were reported, like offering flowers or embracing soldiers. The crowd chanted slogans, kneeled down several times in memory of the dead of Timisoara, and waved holed flags and freshly painted posters. In the meantime, however, the authorities were busy beefing up the security forces by deploying more troops, several water cannons, and armored personnel carriers.

Around 5:00 P.M., the troops began to harass the people, who responded by chanting "Without violence." Suddenly a speeding truck charged into the crowd in the Dalles Hall area, north of the Intercontinental Hotel, causing many casualties. Hundreds of protesters were arrested when they tried to join the demonstration or as they wandered around the crowd. Those in custody were savagely beaten and taken to prison. Around 7:00 P.M., two fire engines split the crowd and splashed it with water. A few demonstrators managed to climb one engine and tried to disable it. The troops then started to fire in the air to scare the people, but the people were unflinching and regrouped at once. They proceeded to build a barricade by using tables, chairs, boxes, and pushcarts from a nearby restaurant. A young man with a megaphone made his appearance around 9:00 P.M. and asked drivers to bring their vehicles into the square to strengthen the barricade. In half an hour several heavy vehicles were brought in, including trucks, minibuses, and a trailer. Two army armored vehicles were blocked.

It was then that the security forces began to try to break the barricade. They first unsuccessfully used the smaller armored vehicles. The demonstrators, who had improvised a strategy of defense, repelled them by setting fire to one of the vehicles, but not before several people were crushed under the caterpillars. Around midnight, an all-out attack against the crowd began, spearheaded by a tank that succeeded, after several attempts, in breaking the barricade that the protesters set ablaze. Behind the tank came the armored personnel carriers and then the troops, shooting first in the air, then on the people. Tear gas grenades were thrown. The clashes continued for several hours. The demonstrators were finally driven away, leaving behind many dead and wounded. Several hundred were arrested.

Battles with the army and security forces took place in some other places, the most serious at the other end of the Balcescu Boulevard, in Romana Square, where people were shot at and some killed.

Goodbye Ceausescu

By early morning on December 22, as the cleaning crews were busy wiping off the blood and the slogans written on the walls and clearing University Square of debris, huge columns of workers set in motion, heading from the outskirts to the center of the city. Those were not the progovernment crowds of the day before, but people determined to get rid of the Ceausescu dictatorship.

In the meantime, inside the party Central Committee headquarters, the last scenes of a pitiful drama were being played. The Ceausescus spent the night in the headquarters. Not much is known about what they did. One rumor had it that the dictator secretly took a ride through the city to see for himself what was going on. He ordered the troops out in force to quench the demonstrations by any means. He convened a final meeting of the party's Political Executive Committee to check once more the loyalty of its members. By presidential decree, a state of emergency was instituted in the whole country because of "the grave violation of public order by acts of terrorism, vandalism and the destruction of public property."

The reading of the decree on the official radio station was immediately followed by an announcement that Defense Minister Vasile Milea had committed suicide, having been exposed as "a traitor of Romania's independence and sovereignty." General Milea was accused of organizing, in collusion with other traitors from within the country and imperialist circles, "all these provocations" and of lying and providing false information about the domestic situation.[17] Few believed this version. (Later it would be seriously challenged but never officially changed.) Whether an assassination or a suicide, one thing seems clear: Milea refused to order his troops to fire on the big crowds that were marching toward the center of the city.

By the time Milea's death was announced on Radio Bucharest, the downtown area was already filled by hundreds of thousands of people demanding Ceausescu's ouster. The army was fraternizing with the people, the *Securitate* was keeping a low profile, and the party and government leadership was paralyzed. Although Elena Ceausescu did not seem to maintain any illusions (having told her younger son and heir apparent Nicu early in the morning that it was "treason from top to bottom"), the dictator was still not ready to give up.

In the square in front of the Central Committee building, the crowd was impatient. The people in the first rows were pressing against the entrance. They wanted to get in. Ceausescu was set to try one final folly: Driven by his insane belief that the people loved him, he decided to get out on the balcony and speak to the crowd gathered in Palace Square in a desperate hope to save himself. The people would not listen. As he was trying to give his speech, an aide approached him, saying that people were beginning to enter the headquarters. He left the balcony in a hurry.

Almost an hour earlier, four helicopters had taken off from the Otopeni air base on a special mission. While in the air, one of them received orders to land at the Central Committee headquarters. There was no space to land anywhere around the building, however. According to the helicopter's pilot, Vasile Malutan, somebody was signaling with a white sheet from the roof of the building.[18] He landed there and waited 20 minutes with the engines on before a group of people finally showed up, among them the ruling couple, virtually carried by their guards to the helicopter. The Ceausescus, two of their closest associates, and two guards occupied all the seats so that the helicopter's mechanic had to sit on Ceausescu's lap. Overloaded, the machine finally took off as the demonstrators were about to get on the roof. The crowd down in the square cheered. Somehow everyone knew the tyrant had fled.

3

The Bloody Aftermath

The ruling couple's flight marked the climax of the Romanian Revolution. Like past revolutions, this one had, for a fleeting moment, gathered around it the consensus of the Romanian people. The universal hate for the Ceausescu dictatorship, the relief, the pride, the bloodshed, the catharsis effected by the explosive nature of the change on a people immobilized for decades by fear and submissiveness created a kind of solidarity in rejoicing and anticipation. It would not last long. What followed was a much murkier mix of suspected conspiracies, street violence, power grabbing, attempts at political and economic reform, electoral experimenting, idealistic striving, and brutal repression. This aftermath raised many questions regarding the revolution itself, its nature, its genuineness, its fulfillment, even its being what it was called all along – a revolution.

"A Real Madhouse"

On December 22, however, the emphasis was on consensus – but consensus about what and around whom? The uprising was largely leaderless. As for a program, a sketchy outline had taken shape with the slogans that the crowds chanted during the demonstrations, first in Timisoara and

44

then in Bucharest. They evolved gradually from general aspirations ("Liberty!") to pointed demands ("We want resignation! Down with Ceausescu!") and then to ingredients of a political program ("We want free elections! We want democracy! We want land!"). Gathering all the aspirations and demands into a well-defined program was not an easy task.

In Timisoara, for example, according to the often-quoted eyewitness accounts, different people at one time or another asserted their leadership of the crowd, giving inspiring speeches or spurring certain actions. No one of them compelled recognition as a leader, however. The columns of demonstrators were constantly changing shape and locations, as they were forced to disperse and reassemble in a different formation and a different place.

A little more cohesiveness was achieved on December 18 and 19. It was only on December 20, however, when all the shooting had come to an end and the demonstrators were in virtual control of the city, that a Popular Democratic Front came into being. This organization put together a program that was read to the crowd. It followed the outline of an earlier draft hurriedly conceived when the crowd's representatives went up to the party county headquarters conference room to negotiate with Prime Minister Constantin Dascalescu.

The situation was quite chaotic in Bucharest on December 21 and on the morning of December 22. As Ceausescu's helicopter was leaving the roof of the Central Committee building, the people demonstrating in the square forced their way into the halls either to search for former officials left behind or out of pure curiosity. Among the demonstrators was Petre Roman, a young, handsome professor of the Polytechnic Institute who would play a major role in the aftermath of the revolution. According to his own account, he and a few others drafted a declaration on behalf of a People's Unity Front that was read from the balcony of the Central Committee building to the crowd outside. "It was drafted as a matter of urgency by four or five people who were there with me," he recounted two weeks later.[1] Several other groups were trying to organize the people, draft programs, or get hold of some prerogatives of power. A participant in these developments later described the atmosphere in the Central Committee building in these words: "It was a real madhouse. Governments were formed one after another, everybody was yelling, everybody was trying to run the palace and the country."[2] Obviously, few were able to make themselves heard, let alone accepted as leaders.

Among the top officials of the former regime who remained in the Central Committee building was Prime Minister Dascalescu. He made an appearance on the balcony, apparently forced by a group of people who took him into custody, to announce his government's resignation and to demand that the troops retreat to their barracks, as ordered. He too had been involved in trying to stay somehow in power as part of a group of Ceausescu's acolytes who asked Ilie Verdet, a former prime minister and member of the top party leadership, to form a new government. Verdet and the people around him were in the process of assigning the different ministerial positions when a group of revolutionaries stormed the room, putting an end to that futile exercise. The Verdet government lasted 22 minutes and was never announced to the public. Verdet appeared on the balcony and attempted to speak to the crowd but was booed and could not finish his speech.

Previously, another Ceausescu henchman, not yet aware of the irrevocable demise of the clique, thought to call upon the younger Ceausescu, Nicu, to succeed his father. This attempt was revealed later by Nicu Ceausescu himself, who at the time was still in Sibiu, where he served as local party boss. He said at his trial several months later that Ana Muresan, a member of the Political Executive Committee, rang him up to implore him to seize power and reverse the outcome of the uprising. Testifying as a witness at Nicu's trial, Muresan admitted making that telephone call but denied having asked the young Ceausescu to take power.

There are few reasons, however, to disbelieve Nicu. The young Ceausescu did not apparently need any begging, but it was too late.

The "Tele-revolution"

In the spacious Palace Square, in front of the Central Committee building, large crowds were enthusiastically engaged in celebrations but knew little about the behind-the-scenes maneuvering. Different speakers addressed them from the balcony, reading programs, announcing the creation of new organizations, blasting the dictatorship, and proclaiming an era of freedom and democracy. Many of the speeches and much of the celebration were carried live by the national television station, renamed the Free Romanian Television. It went live shortly after the Ceausescus' departure, with an emotional broadcast begun with the words: "Brothers! Thanks to God!"Then the dissident poet Mircea Dinescu, one of the best-known and popular opponents of the dictatorship, made the historic announcement in a voice cracking with emotion: "These are moments when God turned his face towards Romanians. Let's look to God! The army in Bucharest is with us. The dictator has run away!"

From this point on, Romanian television would become for several days not only the main source of information for the whole country and much of the world, which was excitedly following what it believed to be the first revolution to unfold live on television, but also, perhaps more importantly, a focal point of the new power to be. Much was made in the Western media about this being the first televised revolution in the history of mankind. In fact, the uprising itself was for all intents and purposes over by the time Romanian television went live. Except for the pivotal moment of the commotion stirred when Ceausescu's speech was interrupted during the support rally he convened on December 21, which was accidentally televised for only a few seconds, the rest that went on television was the aftermath of the uprising and the dubious fighting that followed. Establishing control over television studios and facilities immediately after Ceausescu's fall was one of the deftest moves by the group of dissidents and politicians poised to fill the power vacuum. They defended the television station with great vigor and used it astutely.

The cameras moved constantly back and forth between Palace Square and studio 4 of the television station, where, among many improvised celebrities who managed to grab the microphone and the limelight for a moment, some of the newly important people came to address the nation. Many of those who would become prominent in the postrevolutionary governing bodies paraded before the cameras making statements and announcements. One name came up a couple of times: Ion Iliescu. At least two people invited him to come to the studio. A general in full uniform who was introduced by the name of Nicolae Militaru even gave Iliescu's telephone number and asked the viewers to try to find him and tell him that he was expected at the television station. It did not take long before these invitations were answered.

Iliescu showed up shortly after 2:30 P.M. in studio 4 and was treated with great deference and expectation by those present. The anchorman introduced him with these words: "Esteemed viewers, we have the great joy to host here, in this studio, Ion Iliescu [applause, cheers]. He is the son of a revolutionary and patriot, he himself being a patriot." Giving his first speech, Iliescu displayed astonishing assurance and authority for a person whose official position at that particular moment was that of director of the State Technical Publishing House. He said: "Twenty minutes ago, I spoke on the telephone with General Victor Stanculescu [at that time the acting defense minister]. He is at the Ministry of National Defense. He issued an order. The troops scattered around the city with orders to shoot have been withdrawn. He turned back a column of armored vehicles which had been sent from Pitesti to Bucharest [cheers, applause]. . . . Therefore, comrades, at this moment we have guarantees that the army is with the people."

Iliescu went on to announce that during that same day a Committee of National Salvation would be formed with the aim of restoring order. He called upon "all those responsible people, capable of committing themselves to this constructive work" to come to the Central Committee headquarters at 5:00 P.M., less than two hours from the time of the speech.[3]

Who was this fellow commanding so much respect, getting a full report from the acting minister of defense himself, behaving very much like a leader already in charge before any formal appointment? He obviously was well known not only to those gathered in studio 4, but to a large array of powerful and influential people, including the leaders of the army.

The Virtual Leader

Indeed, for years his name had often been mentioned as a likely successor to Ceausescu at the top of the party and the country, in the event of the collapse of the latter's rule. As the announcer had introduced him, he is "the son of a revolutionary," only of a kind entirely different and opposite to what a revolutionary meant on that day of victory over communism. His father, a railroad worker, was one of the few members of the prewar Romanian Communist Party (RCP). Ion Iliescu was 14 when World War II ended and the Soviet Army occupied Romania. He joined the Communist Youth Union and a few years later was already a leader of the Communist Union of high school student associations of Romania. With his family's Communist background, an extremely rare credential at that time, all doors would open eagerly before him. In 1950, he was sent to Moscow to be trained as a hydroelectric power engineer. There he served as Communist Youth secretary of the Romanian university students attending school in the Soviet capital.

Returning to Romania at the end of his studies, he chose a political career over a technical one and ascended the Communist hierarchy ladder with stunning speed. After serving as chairman of the Communist Federation of Romanian University Students for three years, Iliescu went to work as an official in the Ideology and Propaganda Department of the Communist Party's Central Committee. At 35 he was already a member of the Central Committee itself and head of one of its departments. In the year before that, Ceausescu had taken over the party leadership after the death of Gheorghe Gheorghiu-Dej. Iliescu described the beginning of Ceausescu's regime as "a period full of hope, of opening, that I and the young people of my generation followed with romanticism and a certain enthusiasm."[4] He recalled both the so-called declaration of independence from Moscow and the relative liberalization of the social, political, and intellectual life of the country over several years. In 1967, Iliescu was appointed leader of the Union of Communist Youth and Minister for Youth Affairs, positions that he held until early 1971, when he became secretary of the Communist Party's Central Committee in charge of ideology. He would not keep this job for long.

Ion Iliescu traces his break with Ceausescu to that same year of 1971. He accompanied his boss on a visit to China and North Korea that was to have a great impact on the Romanian ruler's outlook. According to Iliescu, Ceausescu "was literally fascinated by Korea. Much more than by China where an environment of disorder characteristic of the cultural revolution was prevailing. North Korea was the perfect model of an absolute totalitarianism. On our return, he drew up a kind of platform for a cultural revolution Romanian style. That was the break."[5] According to this account, Iliescu declared himself against Ceausescu's plan in a meeting, which prompted the party leader to accuse him of "intellectualism" and to send him for "reeducation" in the provinces. He was appointed party secretary for propaganda in the county of Timis.

That appointment was definitely a demotion, but hardly a break. In three years his political career would move upward again with an appointment as first secretary of the party organization in the county of Iasi. Concurrently, Ceausescu brought him into the highest leadership body of the party, the Political Executive Committee, as a candidate member. The committee was equivalent to the Politburo of other Communist parties, although less powerful because of the excessive concentration of decision making in the hands of the ruling couple and because of its relatively large membership. Iliescu does not seem to have been very influential with the Ceausescus, but neither was he an outcast, a point illustrated by a photograph showing Iliescu relaxing with the Ceausescus sometime during the 1970s, which was enlarged and posted on the wall of the University of Bucharest during the marathon demonstration of April–June 1990.[6] He was brought back to Bucharest permanently in 1979 as head of the National Water Council, a relatively minor government position, and as a member of the Council of State, a sort of presidential council chaired by Ceausescu himself as head of state.

The final blow to Iliescu's political career under Ceausescu came only in 1984, when he was stripped of all his party and government positions, including membership in the Political Executive Committee and the Central Committee (of which he was a part for 19 years), as well as the Council of State and the Grand National Assembly, the nominal parliament of which he was a deputy for almost three decades. He ended up in the minor job of director of the Bucharest State Technical Publishing House, which he still occupied at the time of the revolution.

During the 1960s, Iliescu was seen as a rising star in the hierarchy of the party and then as a reformist alternative to Ceausescu during the 1970s, when the Stalinist traits of the existing regime became all the more obvious. His past position as leader of the Communist Youth movement and his performance in other top party jobs made him a natural candidate for the highest office.[7] Moreover, his acquired reputation as a more relaxed, understanding, and enlightened party boss made him popular both within the party circles and among some parts of the population at large. Such was the case especially in Timisoara and Iasi, where he served in the local party leadership and exhibited a kind of populistic behavior that was in stark contrast to Ceausescu's stiff, arrogant, and authoritarian style.

This reputation may have been enough of a reason for Ceausescu to demote him. In addition, however, Iliescu also passed for an opponent of Ceausescu in secret dealings within the party apparatus. He himself spoke about this in an interview granted to the *New York Times*: "I was somehow known as one who was not in Ceausescu's favor, because I used to express my opinions in a very direct way."[8] The question remains as to what exactly those dissenting opinions were, because they were never made known to the public at the time. As the French newspaper *Le Figaro* put it, Iliescu may have been an opponent of Ceausescu, but never a dissident—that is, someone who took a public stand against the dictator or any of his policies.[9]

In any case, during the afternoon of December 22, he enjoyed considerable recognition and authority. His leadership was accepted with few complaints and no challenge. With a power vacuum to be filled and no other leader or group strong enough to assert power, Iliescu had virtually no obstacle to overcome and no rival to defeat.

Also, there was the army factor. Although withdrawn to the barracks, it was the only organized authority with a structured chain of command. Poet Mircea Dinescu is said to have revealed later that some generals switched sides and joined the anti-Ceausescu revolt only on condition that "serious politicians" took power instead of "a few crazy poets and intellectuals." Dinescu went so far as to assert that "had Iliescu gone on TV one hour later, the revolution would have failed."[10] It is not clear whether the unnamed generals quoted by Dinescu belonged only to the army. At the time, the *Securitate* was far from being disbanded, although some parts of it were in disarray. It is therefore quite clear that any new leader would have needed at least some acquiescence from the army and from sectors of the *Securitate*. Iliescu was apparently able to get it – and perhaps not just acquiescence, but an eager embrace – under conditions that have remained a mystery so far. Mysteries are not conducive to trust; they feed suspicion.

The Videotaped Birth of a New Authority

When Iliescu arrived at the Central Committee building, a number of people were already waiting for him there, among them several former party and government officials disgraced by Ceausescu, known dissidents, active and retired generals, and others, obscure and shadowy associates of the new leader. Surrounded by a select group of people, Iliescu retreated to an office on the second floor. His arrival and the meeting that followed were recorded on a videocassette, apparently at the request of the young revolutionaries who were occupying the building. From their demands, it seems that they were suspicious that Iliescu and the others might try to conspire behind their backs. Right at the beginning of the tape the following exchange takes place:

> *A voice from the crowd:* Film and record everything!
> *Iliescu:* We are going in the large hall to discuss.
> *Another voice:* No! You must talk here. So that we know what is going on. We want to have control.
> *Iliescu:* We want to form a council.
> *A voice:* Yes, but here, my dear. . . . [11]

Iliescu and the others entered the conference room nonetheless. In addition to Iliescu, in that room were initially Petre Roman, the young professor mentioned earlier; General Stefan Guse, deputy minister of defense and army chief of staff; General Nicolae Militaru (retired); and, strangely, some people closely connected to the previous regime, namely Colonel Ardeleanu, the commander of the famous USLA (a Romanian acronym standing for Special Units for Antiterrorist Warfare); Colonel Parcalabescu, national commander of the Patriotic Guards (Ceausescu's civilian troops); and even the two executive secretaries of the dictator, Dumitru Apostoiu and Vasile Nicolcioiu. A little later, two of the signers of the "Letter of Six," Silviu Brucan and Alexandru Barladeanu, joined the others.[12] One or two voices could not be identified.

The videotape is indeed a fascinating document. The French daily *Liberation* called it "an exceptional document." "For the first time in history," *Liberation* added, "a camera could film the birth within closed doors of an insurrectional power." It records a confused and chaotic meeting during which participants speak at the same time, telephone conversations and exchanges between two or more people overlap, and there is constant stirring and little orderly and substantive talk. There seems to be a previously reached agreement about the formation of an interim governing body, but two main issues remain—choosing a name for it and putting the final touches on a communiqué. From the beginning, Iliescu is set to form a Council of National Salavation. A bit later, an unidentified voice objects to the inclusion of the word "salvation":

> *Voice:* Mr. Iliescu, Mr. Iliescu! Salvation is not good. . . . It belongs to a coup d'état. Of National Democracy. . . .
> *Iliescu:* Democracy is with everybody. . . .
> *Voice:* But what does it mean "salvation"?
> *Roman:* Comrade Iliescu, when I spoke there (on the balcony), I said People's Unity Front.
> *Brucan:* It's not good.
> *Militaru:* Call it National Salvation Front, man.
> *Voice:* Democracy, there should be an explicit word.
> *Roman:* Democracy. . . . It has been.
> *Militaru:* Hey guys, the National Salvation Front has been in action for six months, man!

Roman: Democracy Front is not possible because there
was one. . . .
Iliescu: It's a provisional state, until we put together
the new structures of power.
Roman: Of course.
Voice: It creates a state of panic when you say salvation."

The exchanges continue in the same manner for some
time. Iliescu seems to waver. "To tell you the truth, we
should talk some more about the name," he says. We do not
know whether or not they talked again, but the National
Salvation Front surely came into being.

Regarding the issue of writing a communiqué, a version
of it seems to have been already put down on paper by the
time the meeting was convened. It was sent to be typed,
but Iliescu, who apparently had handwritten it himself,
asked, for reasons that remain unknown, that it not be
typed. He was eager to learn other people's ideas, however.
He knew, for instance, that Dumitru Mazilu, a former Romanian diplomat and dissident, had prepared some suggestions, and during the meeting he asked several times that
Mazilu be found and brought to the room.

Mazilu was found only later, after the meeting came to
an end. In fact, he had come to the Central Committee
building about the same time as Iliescu, but they did not
meet. According to his own account, Mazilu was freed
around 2:00 P.M. from a detention place in the town of Alex-
andria, not far from Bucharest, where he had been taken the
night before. His guards brought him back to Bucharest,
and between 5:30 and 6:00 he entered the Central Committee building.

Mazilu went up to the balcony where he read to the
people a program on behalf of a Civic Forum that he subsequently organized.[13] The program had been written by Mazilu, according to his own testimony, between December 17
and 20, as he learned over Western radio stations about the
uprising in Timisoara and became convinced that it was the

end of the Ceausescu dictatorship.[14] Mazilu said that as basis for this program, which was actually an outline of constitutional principles, he used Thomas Jefferson's Declaration of Independence and the French Revolution's Declaration of Human and Civic Rights.

After his appearance on the balcony, Mazilu went with a large number of people, which he later estimated at 200, to Ceausescu's main conference room. A list of 30 people was compiled, containing several of the most prominent dissidents and opponents of the previous regime, to serve as the leadership of the Civic Forum. As he left the conference room, in the halls he met Iliescu, Brucan, and some of the others. At Iliescu's suggestion, he showed his program to Brucan, who jotted a few changes right on the balustrade. Brucan persuaded Mazilu to give up the Civic Forum and join the National Salvation Front, whose first vice chairman Mazilu would shortly become—second in command after Iliescu, who was appointed chairman. The Civic Forum's program, with some minor changes, was to be presented as the front's program, according to Mazilu.

The formation of the Council of National Salvation Front, its membership, and its program were announced by Iliescu on national television. It was presented as an umbrella organization in which practically all those who took a public stand against the dictatorship were included. In fact, the list read by Iliescu on the evening of December 22 was headed by Doina Cornea, Ana Blandiana, Mircea Dinescu, Laszlo Toekes, Dumitru Mazilu, and Dan Desliu, all of whom (except Dinescu) would leave the front in a matter of weeks or months and become its critics or opponents. That evening, however, the new council enjoyed credibility and even moral authority.

Moreover, the 10-point program of the National Salvation Front embraced the widest aspirations for freedom, democracy, prosperity, and independence of the Romanian people. The points included the establishment of a pluralistic democratic system of government; free elections in

April; separation of legislative, executive, and judicial power and the election of the country's leaders for up to two terms (a new constitution would be drafted); respect for the rights of national minorities and guarantees for their full equality with Romanians; domestic and foreign policies based on the needs and interests of the human being; and full respect of human rights and liberties.[15] On economic issues the program displayed a much more hesitant approach, calling for a restructuring of the national economy on the basis of efficiency and profitability, support for small farm production, and reorganization of domestic trade to meet the daily needs of the population, with no word about a market economy or structural reforms. It promised, however, to end exports of food, reduce exports of petroleum products, and give priority to the needs of the people.

It was a promising beginning that raised high hopes among the people and stirred great enthusiasm within the country and abroad. With the Council of the National Salvation Front in place, the power vacuum was filled. Later, the new leaders left the Central Committee building, where their safety was thought to be endangered. New fighting had started in late afternoon, first around the television building, a 12-storied building topped by transmitters and antennas, then around the Central Committee building. Earlier, as the founding meeting of the National Salvation Front was under way, fighting was already raging in the vicinity. It is strange, however, that none of the participants made any reference to it. They did not seem at all worried. Only toward the end, movie director Sergiu Nicolaescu entered the meeting room and told the participants about the possibility of the building being rigged with explosives that could go off at any time. When Iliescu appeared on the balcony of the building to announce the formation of the council, exchanges of fire were illuminating Palace Square. It was unclear who was firing on whom and for what reason. It remains a mystery to this day.

The Terrorists

At first they were called "securisti" (members of the *Securitate*), then "criminals," and finally "terrorists." Dozens of stories were published in the Romanian and foreign press about these presumed members of Ceausescu's personal guard, special forces not subordinated to the *Securitate*'s regular chain of command, taking orders directly from the dictator himself. They were described as physically strong, well-trained and extremely well-equipped fanatics, organized in a sort of medieval military sect with a special oath, tattoos, and occult marks. Some sources talked about children taken from orphanages and brought up as robots, blindly devoted to Ceausescu and ready for anything in the defense of their master. Reports of foreign mercenaries, Arabs or Iranians, fighting alongside the terrorists were abundant in the Romanian and foreign press. All these monsters, the most common version claimed, were unleashed against the people and the new regime to destabilize the country and perhaps try to restore the dictatorship. "The revolution is in great danger," the people were told. The army came out on the streets again, this time to defend the revolution. Many civilians, mostly young people, joined the soldiers in battling the highly elusive terrorists.

Television was at its best. Moving scenes of frenzied fighting, of wild terrorists being caught, of fallen young heroes being buried were shown all over the world. The international community was worried. There was some talk of possible military support for the new regime from the Soviet Union. Western nations, including the United States, nodded approvingly. Humanitarian aid, primarily medical supplies and equipment, was being flown to Bucharest from different foreign countries.

For several days, fierce battles were reported around the Ministry of National Defense, at the television station, at the Otopeni airport, and in the Ghencea cemetery. Hundreds of people died, several times more than during the uprising, and much property was destroyed, including invaluable art works and precious books.[16] Fighting was reported in other cities as well. The nation was united around its new leaders in resisting the enemies of the revolution.

When the fighting ended, people looked around, saw what was destroyed and what was left untouched, who was killed and who survived, and began asking questions. Some of these questions were displayed on fences and walls right in the center of Bucharest or printed in the independent press: "Why didn't they shoot at the balcony?" "How many terrorists were there and from whom did they take orders?" "What happened to the terrorists when the fighting stopped?"

Other developments and revelations would deepen the mystery and multiply the suspicions. The visitor to Bucharest's Palace Square was struck by an unreal sight: the Central Committee building sat there virtually untouched, with no visible sign of damage, while almost all the buildings around it, including the former Royal Palace, which housed the National Museum of Art at the time of the revolution, and the University Library, were destroyed. Anyone visiting the television station, in a different part of the city, could see a similarly shocking landscape: the television building standing majestic with only some bullet holes here and there, while many of the surrounding buildings were heavily damaged or destroyed. What had happened?

One official explanation was that the army was inexperienced in this kind of urban guerrilla fighting and overreacted out of fear or panic. It is not impossible that one field commander would order his tanks to fire on a building from which his unit was being attacked, of course. Yet all of the destruction around the Central Committee building and the television station could not possibly be the work of one frightened commander. It suggested pattern, not accident.

Also, what was the enemy doing? If the terrorists were out to destabilize the new regime, the obvious thing to do would have been to try to kill not just soldiers or civilian passersby, but some of the new leaders. They were easy targets there on the balcony. If the terrorists were out to throw the country into chaos to get the upper hand, then they could have cut the telephone lines, disturbed the power lines, or damaged or destroyed the television transmitters. They did nothing of the sort; nor did they take over any strategic target anywhere in the country.

Were they too few for a large-scale operation? At the time, there were all kinds of stories about large numbers of terrorists ready to turn the country upside down. On December 23, an urgent appeal was launched summoning the people around the television station and the national radio station to defend the buildings against an expected terrorist attack. Large crowds answered the appeal and surrounded the two buildings. They were given no weapons and never had to defend anything against anybody. In an interview in March 1990, three months after the terrorist affair, an army general, recounting the clashes that had taken place in the area of the Ministry of Defense, talked about a "massive attack with an extremely large force" being launched in "successive waves of terrorists."[17] There were also reports of terrorists using helicopters and balloons. These reports were officially denied. Deputy General Prosecutor Gheorghe Diaconescu reported that the terrorists were equipped with electronic devices capable of simulating not only machine-gun fire, but also air attacks.[18]

The government never offered any information regarding the number of terrorists. In August 1990, the first estimates from presumably informed people were offered to the public. In a newspaper interview, Silviu Brucan, a prominent member of the National Salvation Front's leadership in the immediate aftermath of the revolution, said that roughly 4,000 elite sharpshooters, trained in urban guerrilla warfare and armed with the best equipment, were fighting the army. They belonged, according to Brucan, mostly to the *Securitate* school commanded by the dictator's brother, as well as to some of the special antiterrorist units, to the presidential guard, and to the Bucharest security police.[19]

Whether many or few, whatever happened to them? How many were killed or taken prisoners? Where are they now? There are virtually no answers from the authorities. On August 25, 1990, Prosecutor General Gheorghe Robu stated that his office had under investigation 1,456 people suspected of crimes in connection with the revolution. By the date of his statement, only 30 defendants had been convicted, and 69 others were still being tried, including 27 former high party and government officials and 7 *Securitate* generals. All of them had been charged with crimes committed before December 22, 1989. No person accused of acts of terrorism had so far appeared in a court of law eight months after the fighting. According to the prosecutor general, a mere 22 people out of the 622 still under investigation at the end of August 1990 were suspected of "acts of terrorism that resulted in the death or injury of other individuals." Ten of them were under arrest, which suggested that the others were not considered dangerous criminals.[20]

An "Operetta War"?

If most terrorists were not under arrest and were not even under investigation, the question was, why? There are only four possible responses: (1) No terrorists were caught; (2) some were caught but escaped; (3) for some reason prosecution was not desirable; and (4) there were no terrorists.

The first hypothesis does not stand up to scrutiny. Many people witnessed the arrests of terrorists; some could be seen on television, and the military authorities confirmed the taking of prisoners in many instances. Did they escape, or were they freed? No official answer is available, but it is quite unlikely that all could have escaped. Thus, they were freed either because of insufficient evidence for trials or because of a decision to avoid such trials. According to Silviu Brucan, "All [who had been captured] were freed, mostly by *Securitate* officers." Many, he added, fled the country through Hungary and Turkey. The others "are among us." Many opponents of the present regime believe the terrorists were freed because their trials would have been an embarrassment to the country's new leaders. The critics are convinced that the embarrassment would come from the simple fact that there were no terrorists as described during the bloody days of late December 1989. They call the fighting and the clashes that followed Ceausescu's demise an "operetta war," a staged affair in which only the victims were real. According to these critics, this mini-war was meant to legitimize the new power, to give it the aura and the prestige of the savior of the revolution. As unlikely as this theory seemed, it was widely aired in the opposition press and in articles and books published abroad and was accepted in certain Romanian intellectual circles.

A variation of this staged war theory was whispered in my ear in late June 1990 by a highly placed Romanian official. It attributed the staging to the army rather than to the National Salvation Front; the premise was that the army needed to cleanse its reputation, which had been badly stained by its role during the repression of the demonstrations in Timisoara and Bucharest and its late adherence to the revolution. The mini-war allegedly gave it the opportunity both for an ideal about-face and for additionally discrediting its rival, the *Securitate*. Although nothing is impossible, this version should be seen in the context of a campaign to discredit the army, in which the government was said at the time to be engaged.

The controversy is not only about who the terrorists were, but also about who they were not. Respected independent Romanian journalist Petre Mihai Bacanu, for example, concluded after a detailed investigation that the terrorists were not members of Ceausescu's personal guard. This was the so-called Fifth Directorate of the *Securitate*, a body of elite officers and troops in charge of protecting the president, his family, and high-level guests. Had the members of this unit been those who fought against the revolution, one would expect many dead and injured among them. Bacanu found that only one of them had died, but he was declared a hero, having fallen while defending the television station

against the "terrorists." Moreover, the unit, whose headquarters were located across the street from the Central
Committee building, never used its arms against the demonstrators. "This is why in the first hours of the revolution,
at different headquarters and (official) residences no victims were registered either from among the masses or from
the military forces," Bacanu wrote.[21]

The same investigative journalist found that no officer
or other member of the unit was arrested as a result of his
participation in any fighting. In fact, all of them voluntarily
reported to work as ordered on January 7, when they were
taken into custody. They were freed after 46 days. Bacanu
cannot explain why this unit was suspected of being the
source of terrorism even though all its personnel was put
under the army's command and its arms turned over in due
form to the army. As a result of this suspicion, "the antiterrorist operations were directed against mistaken targets,
with disastrous consequences for the population."[22] Other
journalists (of less credibility, however) investigated the
charges brought against other parts of the security forces
and found similar exonerating circumstances.

There was no reaction from the government to these
findings. It is strange and surprising that the government
maintains – in complete, official, and apparently deliberate
silence – this continuing mystery about the terrorists. At
one point during his trial, General Iulian Vlad, the former
head of *Securitate*, asked whether the court would like perhaps to know who the terrorists were. The judge promptly
adjourned. There was a long pause before the court recon-
vened, by which time the defendant claimed that he actually did not know who the terrorists were.

Asked about this issue in an interview, President Iliescu pleaded innocent by reason of ignorance. What he basically said was that he would like to know as much as anybody else who the terrorists were and what happened to
them, but, he added, "it's the most obscure problem."[23] The
president gave a similar answer when I asked him about the
terrorists in early October 1990. If anything, he added to

the mystery by suggesting that the whole truth may never be known. "History will clarify these things one way or the other," he said. "It is possible that some of them will forever remain a riddle." The following exchange ensued:

> "Why can't they be clarified?" I asked. "Who guards these secrets so mightily?"
>
> "It's not a question of guarding them," Iliescu responded. "The secret must be known to be guarded."
>
> "Somebody must know it," I retorted.
>
> "I don't know," he said. "It's possible. I myself cannot name even those who possess all these secrets."[24]

In his interview with *Romania Literara*, he was, however, willing to speculate about their affiliation: "As a rule, we identified them as people of the *Securitate*. There were probably such people as well, but perhaps not only."

Foreign Mercenaries?

"Perhaps not only," says the president. Who else then could the terrorists be—perhaps foreign mercenaries? It would not be too surprising to find out one day that much of the mystery regarding the terrorists stemmed from the role foreign elements played in the fighting that followed the revolution.

At his trial, Ceausescu was asked by the prosecutor, "Who are the foreign mercenaries who fire on the people . . . ? Who brought them and who is paying these mercenaries?" The former dictator answered that it was "another provocation," repeating his line that he would not respond to questions but "in front of the Great National Assembly, of the people." The judge then dictated to the court clerk the following: "He refuses to answer the question who recruited and directed the foreign mercenaries who are presently killing the peaceful and innocent population."

There were many reports from Bucharest and several other cities about Arabs or Iranians fighting alongside the terrorists and being injured or killed. Their number was never known. In the first admission by a former official of the involvement of foreign elements, Silviu Brucan said in the *Adevarul* interview that "the Romanian terrorists received from the beginning help from some foreigners as well, about 30 according to some information, mostly Palestinians, who were undergoing training at Baneasa and other centers of the *Securitate*." What happened to them? "Some of them were killed or wounded," he said. "Their bodies disappeared from the morgue, while those in hospitals, after being operated or having their wounds bandaged, were taken by their comrades and left the country by air."[25]

Additional details were offered in an exclusive interview with the independent magazine *Baricada* by former officials of the postrevolutionary regime who requested anonymity. (By their description, however, they were surely Brucan and Militaru.) They were quoted as saying: "Some terrorists were obviously foreigners. It is not by chance that on December 25, 1989, the first plane that arrived with foreign aid was from Libya. It went back to Libya with a human load. In the total chaos of that time, the new power did not know of the load carried to Libya by that particular plane (that took off from Otopeni at a time when the airport was still closed to traffic)." The same former officials pointed out that the terrorists used Western-made, sophisticated weapons that were not in the Romanian Army's equipment. Such weapons included highly efficient firing systems for operations by night, which explained their preference for night-fighting. They also had a very well-organized system of recovering their wounded and dead. Several wounded terrorists, some of them only slightly wounded, were quickly finished off by their own comrades.[26]

The magazine added its own comments, citing what it believed to be additional evidence of Libyan involvement – namely, the hasty statement made by Libya's ambassador to Bucharest on Romanian television on December 25,

1989, offering his government's recognition of the new power, the first such statement by any foreign ambassador.

During those days, some reports claimed that Libyan warships were approaching Romania's Black Sea coast. At one point, the commander of the naval forces in the Constanta area requested instructions from the army chief of staff about how to deal with foreign helicopters apparently flying toward Romania. The French news agency France Presse carried a statement issued by the office of the commander of the Romanian naval forces, Rear-Admiral Constantin Iordache, citing information received from Soviet and Bulgarian authorities regarding "the presence of suspect ships" 60 miles off the Romanian coast, from which helicopters were sent.[27] Later, Romanian officials denied the report and said that actually there were no helicopters, only electronically simulated flying machines. They have called it "the electronic war" ever since. No official said, however, who waged that war, in what way, and for what purpose. Still, Romanian press reports have continued to insist over many months that foreign helicopters have indeed flown over parts of Romania.

But why would any foreign power come to Ceausescu's succor? They may have had a treaty obligation to do so. During the trial of Ceausescu's four main associates in early February 1990, one of the defendants brought up the subject in public session. Telling the court about how he was interrogated by six prosecutors, sometimes late at night, Ion Dinca blurted the following example:

> During the night of 27-28 [of January 1990] at 12:30 A.M., I was called by several people from the Prosecutor's Office to tell what I knew about the agreement entitled Z.Z. between Romania and five other states providing for the dispatching of terrorist forces to Romania in order to intervene in case of a military Putsch. This agreement Z.Z. is entitled "The End of the End." I stated then, and I am stating now to you, that I have never been involved in this agreement, neither I nor

other people. And I was told: Only you and two other
people know this. I stated that and a detailed check
was made in order to prove that I was not involved in
such acts.[28]

Dinca was not asked to clarify anything, and he did not
volunteer any intelligible explanations. Nor did the government say what that agreement was all about, whether real
or imaginary.

More than seven months later, Constantin Vranceanu,
an investigative reporter for the largest independent newspaper, *Romania Libera*, reopened the subject by quoting a
"prominent political personality who requested anonymity"
and who confirmed that such an agreement was in effect
between Romania, Iran, Libya, Syria, and the Palestine Liberation Organization (PLO). The agreement provided for
each of them to come to the aid of the other with armed
forces in case of disturbances that would endanger the safety of the other country's ruler. The reporter added that this
information was corroborated by certain highly placed *Securitate* people. He writes that, in keeping with the provisions of this agreement, "foreign troops were directed by
helicopters to Romania, flying over Greece and Bulgaria.
Many of these [helicopters] got to Romania, being, in fact,
spotted by radar." The reporter claims to know that the
superpowers, especially the Soviet Union, "put pressure on
the countries involved in the 'Z-Z' plan, forcing them to
renounce any intervention."

It was impossible to check the accuracy of the newspaper report. In any case, U.S. officials profess to know nothing about such a plan. The reporter also quotes one of the
pilots of Ceausescu's airplanes as saying that the dictator
took with him a large shipment of gold ingots on his last
trip to Iran, during the unrest in Timisoara. Vranceanu
wonders whether that might have been the payment for an
armed intervention.[29]

There is no way of knowing whether all this is true or
not. What we do know is that General Piotr Lushev, deputy

chief of staff of the Warsaw Pact, considered Romania to be
under foreign aggression. This is what General Nicolae Militaru, minister of national defense at that time, said in an
interview in May 1990, regarding a telephone call he received from the Soviet general on the evening of December
23. After the Romanian minister briefed him on the situation, General Lushev told Militaru: "It is a matter of foreign
aggression. Romania, don't forget, is part of the Warsaw
Pact. Keep us informed."[30] Whose foreign aggression was it?
Undoubtedly the 30 Arabs that Brucan had talked about
did not amount to an aggression that would worry the deputy commander of the Warsaw Pact.

The postrevolutionary government was reluctant even
to mention the subject publicly. When forced to say something, the officials claimed to have no proof of any foreign
participation in the fighting. When asked by an Arab correspondent at a UN news conference about the rumors regarding PLO involvement, President Iliescu flatly denied
that Palestinians were among the terrorists. When I asked
him a similar question, pointing to Brucan's assertion regarding the Palestinians, the president was less emphatic:
"It's possible that Brucan has more information than myself," he said.

The unofficial explanation for these official denials con-
sisted usually of reminders of the lucrative contracts between Romania and some of the radical Arab countries and
of the many thousands of Romanian workers on temporary
assignment in those countries. Constantin Vranceanu
writes in his previously quoted article that several weeks
after the revolution "the president of an involved country
threatened the Romanian government with reprisals
against the several thousand Romanian citizens working on
contracts in that country if the foreign terrorists are not
returned dead or alive." According to Vranceanu, that blackmail was effective, and a Romanian airplane made a less
than usual flight to a Polish airport, where the even less
usual cargo of able-bodied and injured individuals as well as

coffins was transferred onto another plane that took off to an unknown destination.[31]

Mysteries within Mysteries

In the unlikely event that the mini-war was indeed staged by the regime itself, as many people believe, then it would have been in the regime's interest to manufacture answers to at least some of the many questions raised by the press and the opposition, offer a convenient scenario, put some "terrorists" on trial, and try vigorously to put the issue to rest. Instead, the policy has been the almost ostentatious avoidance of any answers, as though the interest of the present rulers is to keep the mystery alive rather than clear it up. Could this silence be, in fact, a kind of blackmail that keeps certain parts of the army and/or *Securitate* in line and somewhat obedient?

In any case, one mystery may be a key to another mystery. The war against the terrorists was the main reason given for the speedy trial and execution of the Ceausescus. Given the official assumption at the time that the terrorists were still hoping to restore in one way or another the dictatorship and perhaps even bring back Ceausescu himself, it was argued that the dictator and his wife had to be put on trial and executed expeditiously to discourage the terrorists and put an end to the fighting. The intensity of the fighting indeed subsided as soon as the execution was announced. In a day or two, it completely stopped all over the country, supremely vindicating the new leadership's reasoning.

Of course, this version is hotly disputed by many Romanians and foreigners. As long as the nature of the "terrorists" is not categorically established, their objectives remain unknown as well. Therefore, one cannot definitively conclude how important a role they played in the new leadership's decision to dispatch the former ruling couple expeditiously. Logically, if the "terrorists" were not what they were thought to be—namely, die-hard supporters of the Ceausescus engaged in a desperate attempt to restore the old regime—then why would their action be influenced by the former dictator's fate? A more basic question is, why would they hope to reverse the outcome of the revolution if they did not do much to preserve the dictatorship in the first place? It was irrational to engage in a rear-guard hopeless battle when everything was already lost.

In addition, it remains a source of great amazement how miserably these two all-powerful rulers, who had created one of the most fearful secret police in the world, dug elaborate escape routes, and reportedly made precautionary international arrangements for precisely this kind of situation, were forced to flee Bucharest and end up in captivity. The way they were captured, the mockery of their trial, and their hurried execution shed a good deal of light on some subjects of later controversy.

The Free-lancing Policemen

The Ceausescus' helicopter apparently took off from the roof of the Central Committee building with no precise plan. According to Malutan, Ceausescu first told him to fly to Olt, then "better to Dolj," and finally "to Snagov, but don't report anything to the ground." The helicopter landed at the Snagov presidential palace, not far from Bucharest. There Ceausescu demanded that the pilot call the air force commander and request several other large helicopters as well as soldiers to protect them. Malutan made a few calls and found out that no helicopter was allowed to take off. "You find your own way," his superior told him. He lied to Ceausescu, saying that the helicopters were ready, but the people there did not know where to send them. The dictator insisted that he call the base again, but after a few exchanges he decided to take off and head for the Boteni airport, roughly 25 miles west of Snagov. The two acolytes were left behind. Before boarding the helicopter, there was an emotional farewell, with Manea Manescu kissing both of Ceausescu's hands. Malutan turned toward his base, but Ceausescu and his guards noticed the maneuver. Finally, the pilot claimed that the helicopter had been located by ground radar and would be destroyed in a minute or two. Ceausescu got scared and ordered him to land, which he promptly did on the side of the highway not far from Boteni, their destination.

The guards stopped a car and at gunpoint emptied it of four passengers. The driver, Dr. Nicolae Deca, reluctantly took his new load. He dropped them at a gas station where they commandeered another car driven by Nicolae Petrisor, who took the Ceausescus to the Center for Plant Protection, on the outskirts of Tirgoviste, a town about 45 miles northwest of Bucharest. Petrisor said that all the time Ceausescu was looking at his watch and up to the sky. Some sources claimed that he had a beeper in his watch by which his supporters could establish his whereabouts. This claim was never documented, and some knowledgeable people denied it. It seems, however, that the pair was hoping to be saved, although what they had in mind is not known.

It was later disclosed that since 1985 Ceausescu had had a plan to flee the country in case of emergency. One of his planes, a Boeing 707, was always ready for takeoff at Otopeni international airport. According to the previously quoted anonymous former conspirators and high officials of the new regime (most probably Brucan and Militaru), Ceausescu's intention was to have his helicopter land on the Bucharest-Pitesti highway at kilometer 80, where the road's construction permits the landing and takeoff of large aircraft. He was to board the presidential plane on the highway. The destination would have probably been Libya. The Boeing was not ordered into the air as planned, however. The order should have come from the acting minister of defense, General Victor Stanculescu, who, the conspirators claim, brought the helicopter to the roof of the Central Committee building. It is known that Stanculescu led the Ceausescus to the roof and saw them off.[32]

From what is known, neither the army nor the *Securitate* had any plan to recapture the dictator. Unless there was a deliberate attempt to mislead the public (as some analysts have suspected, but for which there was little logical motivation), nobody really followed the movements of the former ruling couple after they were abandoned on the country road by the helicopter. The news offered on national radio and television was contradictory. Reports of their arrest alternated with news of their escape or of their flight abroad to Libya or Iran. No police or security units were alerted in the area where the Ceausescus were dropped off.

According to one eyewitness account, the officers and noncommissioned officers of the Dimbovita county police were watching television when two citizens appeared and excitedly announced that they had been following a black car in which the Ceausescus were traveling to the town of Tirgoviste, but had lost the car somewhere on the way.[33] Nobody seemed interested in the news. It was 1:30 P.M. Half an hour later, a black car stopped at the entrance of police headquarters. A man came out and reported that he took the Ceausescus to the Center for Plant Protection. Again, little interest was shown by the officers. According to the same eyewitness account, the chief inspector said simply: "Silly stuff, don't believe these rumors!" Sergeant Ion Enache and his friend Sergeant Paise Constantin, both traffic policemen, made a decision on their own, however.

The Ceausescus were indeed at the center, a bit frightened. The officers told the couple they had come to protect them and take them to a safe place. After a long drive through the city, where their car was constantly chased by private cars, they managed to get away from crowds and traffic, hiding for some time at the edge of a forest. From the discussion between the couple and the two policemen, it seems clear that the Ceausescus had no idea where to go and how to hide. They kept wondering why the people were so angry at them and hoped to find perhaps a friendlier environment in an army unit or in Petresti, Elena's birthplace. As the dark was setting in, the policemen took to the road again, heading back toward the town. Only when they arrived at the county police headquarters in Tîrgoviste did the Ceausescus realize that they were caught. The two freelancing policemen delivered their catch, unharmed and bewildered, to their commanders.

The official confirmation of the dictator's arrest came the next day from Ion Iliescu himself. At the end of a televised speech, on the afternnon of December 23, Iliescu said: "Finally, comrades, we want to inform you that Nicolae and Elena Ceausescu were arrested and are under military guard. . . . The time will come for their just and harsh judgment by the people."[34]

Execution in a Rush

The time came much sooner than anybody expected, and the people had nothing to do with the trial. In fact they learned of the summary and secret trial, followed immediately by execution, only when the Ceausescus were already dead. It happened on December 25, 1989. When the whole affair was over, the media announced it in a brief news item. Later on, the bullet-ridden bodies were shown on national television.

The controversy began almost instantaneously, somewhat more timidly in Romania, but with great vigor abroad. The summary trial and execution of the Ceausescus cast a shadow on the nascent Romanian democracy. It was not the rule of law that the new leaders had promised their people. Moreover, the secrecy of the trial and the excessive haste in killing the dictator and his wife aroused suspicion that the new leaders wanted to prevent any embarrassing or damaging revelations that the former ruling pair could have made.

The Romanian public was shown carefully selected excerpts from the videocassette recording of the trial and execution. The excerpts were shocking but did not reveal the true dimension of the masquerade. Several months later, the whole video was played on French television. It is not known how the French obtained the cassette. They apparently bought it for cash from a Romanian whose name was not disclosed. The video was hot property in the immediate aftermath of the execution, as President Iliescu confessed to *Romania Literara* in the previously quoted interview (July 5, 1990):

> We were staying in the Defense Ministry building at which shots were directed from the neighboring buildings. We were afraid that [the video] may disappear. There was only one copy. We didn't even trust to lock it in a safe. During that night [of December 25] the film was kept in the room in which I and [Prime Minister] Petre Roman slept, Petre Roman hiding it under his pillow.

Because the television station was pressing to play the video, the two agreed to let television technicians come to the Ministry of Defense and make a copy of the video. According to Mr. Iliescu, the copy shown on French television must have been made during that time, but how it got to Paris was a mystery for the president at the time of the interview. The same tape minus the gruesome final scenes was shown later on Romanian television as well. These scenes would only be shown eight months after the execution.

The trial was nothing but a shouting match between the judges and the accused, with little difference between the prosecutor and the defense counsel. The main charge was that of genocide, in which, the prosecution maintained, 63,000 people died. Other charges included the undermining of the national economy, the use of armed action against the people, and the attempt to flee the country and take advantage of the more than $1 billion allegedly deposited in foreign banks. Nicolae Ceausescu refused to answer many questions, arguing that he, as president of the republic, had a legal obligation to account for his deeds only to the National Assembly. He scornfully rejected the military court as illegitimate. To a few questions he offered some responses; to others he was prevented from answering by the judges. The trial yielded virtually no new information on any subject and few insights on the ruling couple's thinking, their mentality, and their relationship. It confirmed Ceausescu's firm conviction that he was the victim of a treacherous putsch "launched with aid from foreign agents."

The trial also showed Ceausescu's remoteness from the dire realities of the country with such ludicrous remarks as the one that claimed, in response to a question from his accusers on the destruction of villages: "Never was there in the villages as much wealth as there is now. I have built hospitals, schools, no country in the world has such things." A minute earlier he had bragged that "every peasant in this country" had 200 kilograms of wheat "per person, not per family." He thought he was loved by the people and recalled "the great ovation" that greeted him on his visits around the country. He even seemed to take seriously his wife's scientific pretense, retorting to a judge's sarcastic observation by earnestly pointing out that "there are works published abroad," as though he never knew how those works were printed. When the prosecutor cited the fraudulent way in which the first lady, who could hardly read or write, acquired her academic titles, a presumably hurt Elena Ceausescu wondered what her "fellow intellectuals" would say about such an allegation.

"Proof! Show us the proof!" Elena demanded when asked about secret bank accounts. They derided the tribunal, showed contempt, impatience, and a good deal of pride. Nicolae often touched the hand of his wife, talked with her in a whisper, exchanged glances with her. They seemed in harmony with each other, perfect partners in evil to the very end. They dismissed many of the charges in disparagement, with no more than an ironic smile, a gesture of the head or hand, and sometimes with shouts of profanities. Ceausescu often looked at his wristwatch in a sign of defiant boredom or, as some have suggested, with desperate hope.

At no point did the Ceausescus appear to understand that their lives were at stake. They seemed amused at times, certainly more composed than their accusers, behaving with a kind of detachment that, considering the circumstances, was construed by some to be just plain human dignity. Only at the end, when they finally realized that they were going to die, did the Ceausescus lose their composure and succumb to the terror and frenzy of the inevitable execution. Even on videotape the scene is lurid, chaotic, and unbecoming, as much the miserable end of two aging tyrants who tortured their people for a quarter of a century as the awful finale of a judicial masquerade.[35]

The execution itself was never shown and apparently never recorded. The authorities explained that as soon as the two Ceausescus appeared in the courtyard of the garrison where they were tried, the soldiers started to shoot at them in a fury. The cameraman did not have a chance to get out and record the execution. He only filmed the two bullet-ridden bodies, a fact bound to produce doubts and suspicions. Indeed, some French forensic experts have concluded that the final scenes of the film were faked, while in reality the dictator and his wife were killed separately by single shots to their heads and their corpses later propped up for a staged execution by the firing squad. Another version, attributed to an official of the Romanian Ministry of the Interior, has it that the two were killed while being tortured after the trial to extort from them the numbers of their Swiss bank accounts.

There is no way to establish the truth without some convincing evidence. The likelihood of such scenarios seems quite small. Was the trial itself faked? If not, why would the execution be staged? It does not make too much sense, although a firing squad execution may be more acceptable to the Romanian and international public than a KGB-like killing by a single shot to the head.

The serious problem, however, is not with the kind of execution but with the haste and total disregard for due course during the whole procedure. It was a monumental blunder that would weigh heavily on the world's view of Romania's new rulers. Ceausescu's victims – a whole people—will probably never get to know the entire truth: the terrible secrets of this mad tyranny, how it was possible, and who helped perpetuate it for so long. Some of the best words describing the painful frustration that many Romanians felt after the trial and execution were spoken by Paul Goma, well-known Romanian writer and early opponent of the Ceausescu regime. He said that those who hurried to kill the dictator in fact "stole Ceausescu from those who suffered because of him" and by that mockery of a trial "they accomplished the extraordinary, the unheard and undeserved feat of turning the Ceausescus into human beings."[36]

The trial and execution of the Ceausescus could also be viewed as an attempt to channel the wrath of the Romanian people entirely upon them and away from the Communist system itself. It was a kind of final parting with a calamitous era with no deliberate inquiry into the causes and wide range of responsibilities and guilt. Indeed, all the trials that followed, implicating either high-ranking officers of the *Securitate* or close associates of the Ceausescus, dealt virtually exclusively with their complicity in genocide—that is, with their responsibility during the seven days of the revolution—but made little or no reference to their culpability as people who brought Ceausescu to power, maintained him, faithfully executed his ruinous policies, and were in their own right devoted keepers of the Communist system. Although more attention was given to following due course in the later trials, the absurd limitation of charges and lack of any serious digging into the workings and crimes of the Communist regime meant that later trials were no less of a parody rich in punishments and woefully poor in lessons.

The Genocide That Never Was

The Ceausescu trial and the trials that followed have also abused the memory of the fallen heroes of the revolution. The widespread use of the charge of genocide is not only inaccurate but irreverent to the memory of the dead, as was the occult manipulation of the number of casualties in the immediate aftermath of the revolution.

Genocide is defined by the dictionary as the use of "deliberate, systematic measures toward the extermination of a racial, political, or cultural group."[37] There are no essential differences between this definition and that given by the *Contemporary Romanian Language Dictionary*. Ceausescu was accused of the death of 63,000 people. At his trial, the suggestion was that the victims were all killed during the days of the uprising. The estimates of casualties were initially very high indeed, owing to innocent embellishment or deceitful design. In Timisoara alone there were said to be 4,630 dead. A common grave uncovered there was said to contain up to 4,000 bodies of men, women, and children killed during the revolution. Gruesome pictures of those unearthed bodies were shown on television everywhere in the world. No less than 5,000 dead were reported in the Transylvanian city of Sibiu, where Nicu Ceausescu was the local party boss. The dead in Bucharest were numbered in the thousands.

Two weeks after the Ceausescus were executed, a spokesman for the National Salvation Front sharply lowered the number of dead to 10,000. He said that the 63,000 figure cited at Ceausescu's trial comprised all those killed during the 25 years of his dictatorship. Even 10,000 turned out to be a gross exaggeration. The final official data issued by the government in June 1990 set the number of people killed during the seven days of the uprising at an incredible 144, with 727 wounded. The number of people killed during the fighting after Ceausescu's flight was more than six times higher—889, with 1,471 wounded. Of the total of 1,033 dead, more than half were killed in Bucharest. Timisoara follows with 97 dead.[38] These 97 include the 40 bodies that were shipped secretly, on Elena Ceausescu's orders, from Timisoara to Bucharest and incinerated in the capital city's crematory.

This macabre affair took place during the night of December 18–19. The Timis county hospital's morgue held the bodies of 58 people killed during the antigovernment demonstrations who were to be identified and handed over to relatives. Before midnight, however, a group of security officers showed up at the hospital and, in the presence of the hospital's director, loaded 40 bodies into a refrigerator truck. They were taken to Bucharest, more than 300 miles to the southeast, and cremated as soon as the truck got to the crematory. Ceausescu was then in Iran. His wife, who is said to have given the order for this bizarre operation, wanted to destroy the evidence of the massacre or to diminish its extent.

The cry in Timisoara has been ever since: "Where are our dead?" There and in other places critics are not satisfied with the government's accounting of the casualties of the revolution. They believe that although the postrevolutionary power first greatly exaggerated the number of casualties to magnify the revolution and arouse people's support for the new government, it has since played down the human toll to protect the army and the *Securitate*. There is no definitive proof that any intentional manipulation took place. The initial hype could have been a combination of revolutionary fervor and chaotic circumstances. As for the latest data, so far the challengers have not come up with any documented alternatives. Nevertheless, the controversy over the number of casualties is part of a larger set of doubts and suspicions regarding the revolution itself and the very nature of the change that it brought about.

4

Conspiracy, Conspiracies

Assessments of the events of December vary widely. At the one extreme is the exuberant view, which rejects as slanderous any facts or analysis that cast a shadow on the revolution's glory. In this version, embraced at least initially by the new rulers of the country, what happened from December 16 until December 22 and even during the following days was a popular uprising entirely spontaneous, heroic, and uplifting. There were no conspiratorial interferences, no organizational framework, no prior planning, no programmatic guidelines. The revolution succeeded solely by the irresistible surge of popular discontent and rebellion that the army and segments of the *Securitate* were unable to contain and allowed in the final stages to develop and come to fruition.

On the other extreme are several books and articles discarding any idea that the events of December were a genuine popular revolt against the dictatorship. A coup d'état is all there was. Two of the books were published in France. One was authored by Michel Castex, a French journalist who covered the street fighting that followed Ceausescu's downfall for the news agency France Presse. It is entitled *A Lie as Big as the Century: Romania, the History of a Manipulation.*[1] The other book was written by Radu

Portocala, a French journalist of Romanian descent, under a title that says it all: *Autopsy of the Romanian Coup d'État: In the Country of the Triumphant Lie.*[2]

Although there are certainly several less extreme versions to be examined and much information to be analyzed, the fact remains that a final and complete assessment is simply not yet possible. Too many blanks remain to be filled in and too many mysteries to clear up. Moreover, there are powerful vested interests that have attempted to remake history to suit their own purposes. The very legitimacy of the rulers who took power after the uprising was dependent on a certain set of revolutionary circumstances. They and others may have been eager to preserve one version at the expense of another. Politics has also vitiated the search for the truth to some extent. Finally, a taste for the sensational colluded at times with extreme skepticism, yielding questionable results. It is in this context, therefore, that differing versions, conspiracy theories, and contradictory analyses should be viewed.

Lies, Plots, and Sherlock Holmes

Most theories are conceived in definitive terms. Many were initially developed in the West, especially in France. As early as ten days after the demise of Ceausescu, the French television station FR3 put forth the first suggestion that a plot may have been the origin of the Romanian upheaval. Commenting on the videotape made at the founding meeting of the National Salvation Front, FR3 concluded that the front had been in existence long before the revolution and as such plotted an anti-Ceausescu coup for December 24. It asserted, without offering any evidence, that the plotters had to advance the date of their coup by a few days because of the unexpected uprising in Timisoara. This assertion made the front pages of some Romanian and foreign publications, but a fully developed conspiracy theory would not come to light until late May 1990, when the French magazine *Le Point* carried a long and sensational article purporting to unveil the truth about the uprising. It denounced "the deceptions of a change of power that was as much a popular revolution as Potemkin's villages were authentic." In fact, according to *Le Point*, "the Romanian affair was a plot prepared by the communists and guided by the Soviets. Its purpose was to replace a communist dictator who lost his decent appearance by a regime with the imprint of Perestroika."[3]

In essence, but with different emphasis and degrees of subtlety, most conspiracy theories contend that there was a plot with Soviet connections. The most splashy of all is the earlier mentioned book *A Lie as Big as the Century* by French journalist Michel Castex. The writer, who headed the Agence France Presse team assigned to cover the Romanian scene after Ceausescu's flight (he arrived in Bucharest on Christmas Day), uses an entertaining mix of personal memories, selective information, and hearsay in flamboyant style to lead the reader through a maze of facts and circumstances to a preannounced conclusion: There was no revolution, only a staged intoxication of the media and the public to make them believe a genuine popular uprising had taken place where there was only a banal putsch. He devotes a great many pages to unveiling the alleged manipulation of the media, of which he was himself both a conduit and a victim. In the final pages he enlists Sherlock Holmes himself to sort out the truth, happily and squarely confirming the writer's surmise of a conspiracy led by a *chef d'orchestre* revealed, with the unfailing logic and certainty of the famous detective, to be Mikhail Gorbachev in person.

While reaching basically the same conclusion, Radu Portocala's *Autopsy of the Romanian Coup d'État* takes the narration several steps further in both chronology and content. It is forceful, penetrating, and imaginative. At the beginning of his work, the writer rightly asks the annoying question, "Is it possible, with a lapse of less than one year, to make the journalistic and historical dissection of an event whose origins and scope are international, and which, by its very nature, is mysterious?" He continues quite unassumingly: "Can, at least, more modestly an attempt be made to examine the elements at hand, to ask the right questions, to search for logical answers and to reset the whole in a context of truth?" His answer is emphatic: "It's a necessary undertaking."[4] So it is. The trouble is that from that point on, the author describes his own version of the events, rarely making the critical distinction between established facts, whispered rumors, and personal suppositions.

One of his contributions is to expand the list of villains to include the United States and, to a lesser extent, other countries, at least as accomplices of the Soviets. The essence is captured in the following quotation:

> In all this development, note must be taken of the active inattention of the Americans, who played into the hands of the Soviets in Romania. . . . 1988 is the year when Soviets and Americans abet the work of the dissident movement and strengthen its reputation. Moscow continues the discreet writing of the scenario; the West provides in a noisy manner the link with the country via the radios that broadcast in Romanian – Radio Free Europe and the Voice of America, belonging to the United States, which are joined by the British BBC. These radios will be, until the end of the events, the more or less voluntary resonance boxes of the [Soviet] conspiracy.[5]

Those among the book's culprits (it is unclear whether the author considers himself to be one of them because he served at the time as the Voice of America's Paris correspondent, broadcasting in Romanian) must try hard to imagine what regret is expected of them: is it perhaps that they should not have supported the opponents of the regime and instead aided Ceausescu in resisting the suspected Soviet plot to topple him?

The absolute extreme is attained by an ultranationalist Romanian publication. Its list of foreign intelligence services involved in inducing the revolution extends way beyond the KGB and CIA to include the Israeli Mossad, the Hungarians, the French, and the British, as well as the so-called fifth column (the Hungarian population of Romania).[6]

If one were to believe all these versions, it would seem that the whole world conspired to effect what must have been, after all, the most obvious and imminent change of all. It did so by resorting to a large array of bizarre (and despicable) tricks to arouse a population whose hatred for its tormentors should have been (and in fact was) unequaled in the whole of Eastern Europe.

The Moscow connection is also prominent in a different kind of book, *The Unfinished Revolution: Romania between Dictatorship and Democracy*.[7] Author Anneli Ute Gabanyi, a West German analyst of Romanian origin, analyzes in detail some of the more shadowy facets of the revolution to reach a controversial conclusion, although with some nuances and reservations that make it a worthwhile exercise. The author herself summarizes this conclusion as follows:

> What happened after December 21 (or perhaps even beginning on December 16) was a putsch, a coup d'état prepared over a long period of time by several groups and circles interested not so much in a change of regime as in a transfer of power to a counterelite with a different stance toward the Soviet Union from within the Romanian Communist Party, the army and the *Securitate*; an internationalist pro-Soviet group.[8]

The Soviet factor is certainly one that must be dealt with and clarified as much as the available evidence allows it, but the evidence is sketchy and virtually all circumstantial. It must be (and will be) examined in the general context of the revolution and its enigmas.

Of course, all these writers have been preceded by none other than Ceausescu in advancing the idea of a coup masterminded or supported from abroad or serving foreign interests. As we already noted, he first suggested it, then stated it directly, and repeated it several times during his trial. He shouted it to his judges before being led to his death, in a kind of last word and final testament. The fact that Ceausescu himself believed that he was the victim of a foreign-inspired conspiracy (although he was remarkably reluctant to name the Soviets specifically as instigators, sponsors, or participants) is not credible proof one way or the other, however. In fact, it has been used on both sides of the controversy. Those believing in a conspiracy by foreign agents claimed that Ceausescu must have had access to secret information that made him fear a putsch. It is not known what that information was. If indeed he had any credible evidence, he took it to his grave. Postrevolution officialdom, on the other hand, labeled suggestions of a foreign-engineered coup as "the Ceausescu version," trying to discredit it by simply linking it to Ceausescu, known for many years for his neurotic suspicions.

The Brucan-Militaru Version

It is possible that Ceausescu was the target of a locally concocted plot or plots, painstakingly developed over many years. There are several testimonies from different sources about such a plot, but one in particular, coming from two of the major self-described conspirators, is of great interest. After a long wait and repeated denials, Silviu Brucan, initially the *éminence grise* and ideologue of the National Salvation Front, and (retired) General Nicolae Militaru, the minister of defense in the postrevolutionary government, acknowledged publicly on August 23, 1990 that sectors of the army and the *Securitate* had been already won over by a conspiracy against Ceausescu by the time of the popular uprising. Although they took great care not to belittle the uprising and did not specifically say that Ceausescu was ousted by a palace coup d'état, the clear implication was that the removal of the dictatorship would have been quite unlikely without the conspiracy. It was because of it, they contended, that a civil war and a bloodbath were avoided.

Brucan and Militaru also claimed that their diligently forged organization in the army and the security police made the relatively smooth change possible on December 22, 1989. Said Brucan:

> The idea that this 180-degree change would have been made spontaneously is entirely mistaken. And he who believes such a thing does not understand what a military structure, fortified over more than two decades, means. In short, the dissident work within the army fully proved its political usefulness and its decisive role in preventing a bloody massacre in the whole country.

Moreover, the fact that the demonstrators in Palace Square could enter the Central Committee building on the morning of December 22 without resistance, thus forcing Ceausescu to flee in a hurry, was also the plotters' doing, according to Brucan. "General Militaru managed to establish contacts with the battalion serving as security guard at the [Central Committee] headquarters, as well as with those doing the same thing at the Council of State palace [the former Royal Palace]," said Brucan.[9]

The suggestion is obvious: The plotters were instrumental in bringing the popular revolution to fruition. Nonetheless, they also admitted that the plot and the popular uprising developed separately from each other. "We never succeeded in establishing a link between the conspiracy and the rebellious masses," Brucan said, although "we conceived the conspiracy as part of the popular revolution and not just as a simple military coup."

Two questions come to mind. First, was it then a putsch by which the conspirators took power? Second, if the plotters were not able to establish a link with the rebellious masses, how could they claim to represent these masses? Based on Brucan and Militaru's testimony, the answer to the first question is "yes," and indeed some journalists and analysts stressed the coup suspicion with no reservations.[10] As for the second question, it goes to the root of the legiti-

macy problem with which the new rulers were sharply confronted from the very beginning.

What we read in *Adevarul* starkly contrasts to what the
same two people, among many others connected with the
new regime, said immediately after the revolution. Brucan,
in particular, strongly and repeatedly denied that the National Salvation Front's regime was anything else but an
outcome of the popular revolution, as did President Iliescu
himself many a time. Back in January 4, 1990, Brucan expressed this view eloquently:

> If the so-called plot organized by the front and the
> army had been true, we, its leaders, would have had
> every reason to boast about it from the very beginning.
> To be in the position of telling the Romanian people
> that Ceausescu had been overthrown as a result of a
> conspiracy planned well-ahead would have been a terrif-
> ic asset for us, a great historic merit that would have
> earned us the people's warmest congratulations. Why
> be so modest and not claim such a great historical
> achievement?[11]

Indeed, why this uncharacteristic modesty? Brucan explained in no uncertain terms that there was not and there
could not be such a plot under Ceausescu. "The truth is," he
said in January 1990, "there never was such a plan. The
making of such a plan under Ceausescu's police state would
have been impossible. Surveillance was so effective that no
political group could possibly take shape inside the party or
outside it, and even less so to involve the military. The
revolution was 100 percent spontaneous." It is interesting to
note that President Iliescu argued against the idea of a
conspiracy in almost the same terms. In his interview with
Romania Literara, he said that there was a long distance to
go from discussions about forging an opposition movement
to organized action that could lead to the removal of
Ceausescu. "If this would have taken the actual form of an
organized action, it would have established a great merit in
history [for the plotters]. There would have been no reason

of embarrassment to reveal such a deed of great courage. Unfortunately, however, such a thing did not happen."[12]

It seems obvious that political expediency must have been the reason why they denied the putsch in the first months after the revolution – in fact, a kind of conspiracy to cover up the conspiracy. The new leaders probably decided that they would rather be seen as an upshot of a popular revolution than as a gang of conspirators plotting for years to grab power from the dictator. They certainly presented themselves as people propelled to power by the will of the rebellious masses, as leaders whose legitimacy was bestowed upon them by the genuineness of the revolution and whose authority stemmed from its ideals. The question is whether Brucan and Militaru's August confession was induced by a desire to tell the truth or again by political opportunism. Both of them were stripped of their influence and power by Iliescu, Militaru soon after the uprising and Brucan a little later. Both must have resented it. Brucan had spoken up a few times and, by summer 1990, had become openly critical of Iliescu. The revelations, therefore, may not have been totally disinterested. It makes one wonder when did they talk honestly: when they denied any putsch or when they revealed it? Their word alone may not be sufficient to establish the whole truth.

In any case, President Iliescu challenged them promptly without, however, discussing any of the details. His main argument was that only "a genuine social explosion" could have toppled Ceausescu. In a commentary published by the same newspaper *Adevarul*, the president said: "If we speak of conspiracy, we may just as well speak of several conspiracies. From a certain point of view the entire people, deeply dissatisfied with worsening social and economic life, was part of a huge conspiracy against Ceausescu." This kind of vague and general statement was both a way to avoid his being dragged into the controversy and a line of defense in case the coup version took hold with the Romanian and foreign public. The president's was a two-pronged strategy: first, to try to present the revolution as an all-out assault against the dictatorship with several different but harmoniously integrated components, none of which alone could bring about the downfall of the dictatorship, least of all a military conspiracy; and second, to depict Brucan, Militaru, and others who openly talked about their involvement in the plot (or plots) as egotists who would go to any length to focus attention on their own role and merits. Iliescu has indeed called on Brucan and others to show more "decency and modesty" in discussing their opposition to Ceausescu, implying they were trying to take the credit for the dictator's overthrow.[13]

A Tale of Two Fronts

Nevertheless, what Brucan and Militaru disclosed has been suspected by many analysts for some time. Moreover, there was ample previous testimony about the plot in its earlier stages from at least two other conspirators – former General Stefan Kostyal and retired Commodore Radu Nicolae.[14] Militaru himself had earlier provided, both voluntarily and involuntarily, information about the same conspiracy, not all of it accurate or consistent with what others had said. In fact, the first speculation ever about a possible coup that had stolen the revolution was triggered to a large extent by a casual remark made by Militaru during the taped initial meeting of the National Salvation Front. He said then that "the National Salvation Front has been in action for six months." Many concluded that the front was not established on the evening of December 22, as its leaders have claimed ever since, but several months earlier, a supposition that was prominent in several conspiracy theories.

Indeed, a National Salvation Front made known its existence several months before the revolution by sending three letters to RFE, of which two were broadcast. The first, read over RFE on August 27, 1989, was an appeal to the delegates to the 14th Congress of the Romanian Communist Party and included a critical analysis of Romania's situation at the time. It called upon the delegates to the congress not to reelect Ceausescu as secretary general of the party. It had a certain international impact, being subsequently published by French newspapers as a letter that originated within the Romanian party nomenclature.

When RFE received the letter, it immediately stirred a controversy over who was actually behind it. For one thing, it was delivered through unusual channels, which made it impossible to verify even if it originated within Romania.[15] Yet, about a month earlier we had been advised from Romania that a letter written by people connected with the Romanian Communist Party's Stefan Gheorghiu Academy was being sent to the radio for broadcast. At first, we were tempted to think that the letter signed "National Salvation Front" could have been the one expected from the party academy. After taking a close look at the letter, however, RFE experts concluded that it was unlikely to have come from within the party hierarchy.[16] The second letter arrived more than 10 weeks later and confirmed the experts' judgment. It was a kind of open letter to Ceausescu asking a number of pointed questions about the economic and human disaster that the dictator had created and his abuse of power. It was broadcast on November 8, 1989.

Several months after the revolution, a professor of the University of Bucharest by the name of Alexandru Melian claimed that he was in fact the author of the letters and that there was no real organization behind the name.[17] That assertion is questionable, however. According to the person who brought the letters to RFE, the first of them was smuggled out of Romania by a medical doctor who claimed to be part of a larger group. The second letter was handwritten by the same doctor while visiting with a relative in Hanover, West Germany.[18] If all this is true, then the inference must be that Professor Melian's claim of authorship may have been false. Why he would make such a claim is anybody's guess.

Whoever is right, it seems fair to conclude that there is no evidence that the National Salvation Front created on

December 22, 1989 had anything to do with the namesake underground group that sent the letters to RFE. This conclusion does not necessarily prove, however, that President Iliescu indeed chose the name, as he put it, simply because he liked it and thought it most appropriate for the body that took power in the moment of grave crisis in which Romanian society found itself on December 22, 1989.[19] Commodore Radu Nicolae, who gave a detailed account of what he knew of the conspiracy in several interviews and a press conference, talked about the formation in February 1985 of a Council for National Salvation, of which he was a member. It is not clear how long this council was in existence. None of the others mentioned it.

To be sure, the whole issue of whether or not the National Salvation Front had the same name before the revolution has lost much of its relevance. After all, does it matter what name the conspiracy used? The circumstances of its existence and the extent of its actual influence may be of much more interest for both the past and the present.

The Onset of the Conspiracy

In the immediate aftermath of the revolution, General Militaru was a great deal less emphatic than others in denying that the overthrow of Ceausescu was the result of a plot. He had even hinted at such a plot in an interview with the French magazine *Le Nouvel Observateur* back in May 1990: "Over the years," he said, "we have prepared a coup d'état against Ceausescu. Everything was ready for the beginning of Spring 1990, but the revolution broke out before Christmas. It took us by surprise. Then we joined it."

Militaru described in some detail the conspiracy in which he and several other military men and civilians were involved for many years. According to this confession, the idea of an anti-Ceausescu conspiracy was planted in his mind in 1974 by then Prime Minister Ion Gheorghe Maurer during a walk in a Bucharest park. Maurer sent away the security people who accompanied him and broke loose against the leader: "I cannot work any more with this fool! He listens to nobody and is ruining the country's economy." The discussion went on for more than two hours. Maurer told Militaru: "I am too old. But if you and several others want to try something. . . . " The former general confided to the French magazine that it was then, on the park bench, that he decided to do his best for a change.

The next episode that Militaru referred to in the same interview took place in a hospital in 1982, when he met Ion Iliescu on the corridor: "I knew his ideas, he knew mine. I asked him: Is it that the needed forces to corner this guy are missing in Romania? Iliescu responded: One must surely consider this. We'll be seeing each other again. That was the beginning of our clandestine work," Militaru said. In 1984, after the general had been retired from the army, the two were seeing each other at least once a week. The group of conspirators had been expanded with the addition of former Minister of Defense Ion Ionita and several others. Another member of the group was Virgil Magureanu, a professor of scientific socialism at the party's Stefan Gheorghiu Academy and a member of the *Securitate*.[20]

Militaru did not say who initiated the formation of the clandestine organization. Retired Commodore Nicolae fills this gap by indicating that the group was initiated by a few university professors at the beginning of the 1970s. In 1970, he said, "I was approached by Professor V. Magureanu who, after several preliminary meetings, suggested that I join an anti-Ceausescu organization conceived by a few academics who sensed the imminent end of Ceausescu's policies. I accepted." Between 1970 and 1982, Radu helped recruit several people for the organization from within the army, the *Securitate*, and the party hierarchy.

One interesting piece of information that the retired navy officer provided concerned the inner working of the organization. According to his account, at the beginning of the 1980s, when the first concrete plans to overthrow Ceausescu were made, there were two groups — one for the military, headed by generals Ionita and Militaru, and the other for the *Securitate*, headed by Magureanu and Iliescu. Radu claimed to have served as liaison in the uneasy relationship between the two groups.

Another account (the earliest of all) spoke about two parallel groups (one of which was Militaru's and Iliescu's) that merged in 1984 and began plotting Ceausescu's ouster. The other group included former Minister of National Defense General Ion Ionita; Janos Fazekas, an ethnic Hungarian and former member of the top party leadership; and the author of the testimony, General Stefan Kostyal, former deputy head of the army's Political Directorate. Each member of the group had people "ready to go into action when the right moment came."[21] In more recent statements, General Kostyal claimed that the *Securitate* group was actually spying on the plotting generals rather than cooperating with them. According to this version, the head of the group was Virgil Magureanu, who "was acting on orders from the disinformation and diversion department of the Securitate."[22]

The 1984 Aborted Coup

According to Nicolae Militaru, an anti-Ceausescu putsch was contemplated as far back as the mid-1970s by then Minister of Defense Ion Ionita and General Ion Gheorghe, chief of staff of the Romanian Army. Militaru and others he did not name argued, however, against a coup on the grounds that a popular uprising was not likely then, the circumstances not having "ripened." With the worsening of the economic, social, and political circumstances in the 1980s, the prerequisites were there. The plotters had observed that during the absence of Nicolae and Elena Ceausescu from the country, the entire party and state apparatus was paralyzed. They were able to obtain well in advance the list of scheduled foreign trips by the ruling couple through a top official named Ioan Ursu, one of Elena Ceausescu's close advisers.

By 1984, the planning of Ceausescu's overthrow was under way, the putsch being set for October 15–17 of that year, when the ruling couple was scheduled to make a state visit to West Germany. According to Commodore Radu Nicolae, the conspirators set out to execute the putsch without casualties. Therefore, they wanted to procure a certain kind of pistol that did not kill the victim but just put the person to sleep. When the Soviets refused to furnish those pistols, the plotters asked the Romanian ambassador to Turkey, Vasile Patilinet, to procure such equipment on the open market. He bought a number of grenades that could temporarily blind and paralyze the victims.

The coup never happened, however, because the mechanized unit of the Bucharest garrison on which the plotters relied was sent to the countryside "for agricultural work." Kostyal was convinced that the plan of the putsch had been "leaked" to the authorities. Brucan and Militaru also expressed their belief that the plotters were betrayed. Nicolae even named the traitors – Generals Gomoiu and Popa. As a result, Kostyal was taken into custody and kept under house arrest in a provincial town. Ionita and Militaru were investigated by two of Ceausescu's closest aides. Apparently, those who gave them away did not know all the details of the plan, a possibility that explains why their only punishment was an interdiction against seeing each other again. Later, however, General Ionita, Ambassador Patilinet, and his son died in dubious circumstances and are believed to have been assassinated by Ceausescu's secret police.

What Drove Them?

These highly placed people put their lives on the line over a long period of time. To assess their endeavor requires knowing them and their motivation. First, they were all dissatisfied Communists. They all served the Communist Party faithfully, some even in the "underground" before and during

World War II. All of them started their careers during Ceausescu's predecessor Gheorghe Gheorghiu-Dej, most having been placed in high positions by Ceausescu. At least three of them had been personally or professionally very close to the dictator at one time or another. General Ion Ionita had been Ceausescu's boss and General Stefan Kostyal his immediate deputy when the future leader served on the Political Directorate of the Romanian Army in 1949.[23] According to former General Ion Mihai Pacepa, head of the Romanian Intelligence Service who defected to the United States in 1978, Ceausescu resented Ionita because Ionita would not treat him with the expected reverence, instead using the old familiarity from the time their roles were reversed.

As secretary of the Central Committee, Vasile Patilinet was also very close to Ceausescu, who entrusted him with the supervision of the army and *Securitate*, one of the most sensitive positions in the party hierarchy. All three were demoted in the 1970s — Kostyal in 1970, Patilinet in 1974, and Ionita in 1978. Pacepa says he was present when Ceausescu summoned Ionita and let him know that he was being "promoted" to the position of vice premier and minister of transportation, which was in fact a demotion. Still according to Pacepa, Ionita tearfully begged Ceausescu to rescind his decision, but to no avail.

The more dramatic case was Patilinet's. Pacepa recalls that in 1973 or 1974, while Patilinet was on a trip abroad, his daughter had an illegal abortion and died during surgery. (Abortions were banned as part of the demographic policies of the Ceausescus.) Unmoved by Patilinet's tragedy, the Ceausescus were enraged that the daughter of a close aide would break one of their most cherished laws. Pacepa was ordered to send a special plane to Cairo to bring Patilinet back. The Ceausescus summoned Patilinet immediately upon arrival and, instead of expressing sympathy for the loss of his daughter, scorched him terribly. Elena Ceausescu was particularly harsh with him. It was a furious discussion, as Patilinet was overwhelmed with grief and had no patience for the ruling couple. After the funeral, Patilinet was dismissed from the Central Committee secretariat and appointed minister of forestry, a minor government job.[24]

General Militaru is more enigmatic. In his book *Red Horizons*, Pacepa describes Militaru in unflattering terms, portraying Militaru as a Soviet spy caught red-handed. It is a story of sex and espionage, starring a certain Olga, who used to be Militaru's girlfriend back when the general was studying at the Military Academy in Moscow. They met again in a Bucharest restaurant, reminisced about their common past, and were then joined by another old pal from Moscow, Vanya, who had just been appointed military attaché at the Soviet Embassy. Vanya wanted a favor from Militaru, who was commander of the Bucharest Military Region at the time – namely, he wanted the top secret General Staff telephone book for two or three days. According to Pacepa, the general acceded to his friend's request and then took Olga in his car to a motel where they spent the night making love. This event happened in 1978, just before Militaru was scheduled to be promoted to deputy minister of national defense – a promotion that was not to happen.[25]

Militaru himself acknowledged that he contacted the Soviets with specific requests for the conspiracy but denied ever spying for them. In his interview with the French magazine *Le Nouvel Observateur*, the retired general glossed over Pacepa's story with a joke: "Can you see me in bed with a Soviet female agent?" He accused the former intelligence chief of concocting the charge of espionage.

It is a fact that, four years later, Militaru was appointed deputy minister of industrial construction, a sufficiently important position to sow some doubt about the seriousness of the espionage charges. Pacepa explains, however, that Ceausescu always avoided convicting anybody for being a Soviet spy. He would either simply neutralize them or convict them on some other trumped-up charges. Even in the celebrated case of General Ion Serb, who was proved to have been recruited by the KGB, an espionage trial was avoided. Instead, he was convicted for violation of the state secret laws and sentenced to a seven-year prison term. After three years, Serb voluntarily confessed about his work for the Soviets and was freed and appointed director of a state farm. Militaru's family connection, as brother of a top party official close to the ruling family, may have induced Ceausescu's leniency, Pacepa believes.

The other military man prominently featured in this affair is Commodore Radu Nicolae, an expert in missiles and submarines. Trained in Romania and in the Soviet Union, Nicolae was a top commander in the Romanian naval forces until 1970, when he was dismissed on the grounds that he criticized Ceausescu's policies. It was during that year that he joined the conspiracy, in which, according to his statements, he played a major role as liaison between the army and the *Securitate* factions. Later he served in important positions in the merchant marine. In 1983, he again got in trouble with the regime and was retired the next year. In 1987, during a search at his home, the security police reportedly found thousands of anti-Ceausescu leaflets. He was sentenced to a 10-year prison term but spent less than a year in jail, benefiting from a general amnesty. He said he was afraid to resume his links with the other conspirators after being freed from detention and did not know how the organization fared and what it did subsequent to his arrest. Another member of the conspiracy, General Stefan Kostyal, expressed great doubts about Nicolae's genuine adherence to the plot, considering him a tool of the security police.[26] As though to confirm this charge, the former naval officer engaged himself in dubious activities on behalf of some of the former Ceausescu acolytes, including the former head of the *Securitate*, General Iulian Vlad. He has allied himself with the ultranationalist groups with strong links to the former security police and uttered the most vicious anti-Semitic attacks of the postrevolutionary period. Moreover, Nicolae expressed disdain for the revolution, embracing the most extreme, *Securitate*-inspired version of the events of December 1989.

All these people certainly had the drive and personal

motivation to turn against Ceausescu. Still, was it just ran-
cor and intimate hatred for Ceausescu that brought them
into this conspiracy? Or was there perhaps also a political
and patriotic dimension to their commitment? Personal
hostility or vindictiveness is probably a necessary, but not
sufficient, ingredient in a sustained, long-term conspiracy.
Such an enterprise requires a strong and dangerous commitment that perishable sentiments are unlikely to sustain.
It is therefore quite possible, indeed probable, that most of
the plotters must have been motivated by a belief that they
were saving the country from a nightmarish dictatorship.
Aside from this general conviction, it is hard to identify a
coherent program of the group. Indeed, most of the participants, with less than a handful of known exceptions, were
military men unversed in politics.

The Ideologue

Enter Silviu Brucan, an astute expert in political science, a
seasoned politician, and a strong personality, one who
thrives on controversy and loves to cast himself in sardonic
roles. Brucan joined the Communist movement as a teenag-
er in the late 1930s.

In 1944, at the end of World War II, he was among the
new breed of Communist propagandists, rising as high as
acting editor in chief of the party daily *Scinteia* in the early
1950s. ("I am horrified when I read what I wrote in those
years," he would confess more than 30 years later, in an RFE
interview.) Appointed ambassador to Washington (1956–
1959) and then permanent representative to the United Nations (1959–1961), Brucan spent many years in the United
States, a country for which he had harsh words of criticism
and even disdain at the time, but where he established good
connections and would return several times during the following decades.

After three years as vice chairman of the State Radio
and Television, Brucan's political and diplomatic career

came to an abrupt halt with Ceausescu's ascendancy to power. This halt may have been simply coincidence or the result of irrelevant circumstances. Yet Brucan suggested a political incompatibility between himself and Ceausescu, claiming to have been among those party people unhappy with Ceausescu's appointment as head of the party leadership. "Although it did not manifest itself immediately, the anti-Ceausescu dissidence began at the very moment of his appointment as Secretary General of the party," stated Brucan in August 1990, presumably including himself in this dissident group.[27]

There is no independent confirmation of his early stand. In any case, he took up teaching Marxism at the university level and writing books. He traveled unimpeded in the West, often to the United States, where he published, supposedly with the Romanian government's approval, several books and articles and taught in U.S. universities.[28] In more recent years, however, in some of his articles and books published abroad Brucan expressed unorthodox opinions, usually regarding socialism in general. Apparently displeased, the Romanian authorities began to restrict his travels.

Brucan first contacted Radio Free Europe in 1986 about some of his troubles with the government and asked for help in obtaining permission to travel (help that RFE provided). He was not yet ready to take a public stand against the dictatorship, however. His first direct public criticism of the Ceausescu regime came in reaction to the November 1987 workers' demonstration in Brasov. Less than a year later, he was, however, allowed to travel again to the United States.

While in New York in 1988, he granted RFE a wide-ranging interview that became one of the major documents of the anti-Ceausescu dissidence within the RCP. I met him then for the first time in person, although we had spoken several times on the phone before. He struck me as a poignant, sometimes abrasive, personality with a commanding intellect. In his interview, he bitterly complained about the regime's "political sectarianism," whereby anybody who thought differently was treated with intolerance, and the leader's "ideological and political monologue stifles the party's life and condemns Marxism to stagnancy." His compelling economic and political analysis went occasionally beyond Marxism, even though his language was (perhaps intentionally) chosen from the Communist vocabulary. "History teaches us," he said, "that a nation which ceases to think ceases to exist or, in any case, hopelessly trails behind other nations." That fate was clearly what he feared for Romania. "If we continue on the same path," Brucan warned, "Romania will be the first country in the world to deliberately plan its underdevelopment for the year 2000," when the nation may find itself in "a neocolonial status." Departing from Stalinist dogma, he emphasized the role of the individual in a modern economy and pointed out the irrelevancy of the state, which had become, in fact, an obstacle to progress. He went on to conclude that "the economic reform must be accompanied by political democracy."

Whether or not he was already part of a conspiracy to overthrow Ceausescu, as it is now suggested, Brucan's avowed objective at the time was limited to "a dialogue between the power and the civil society." As a lifetime Communist and Marxist theoretician, he was worried for what he called "the fate of socialism," which he saw "hanging in the balance." He displayed optimism, however, that "the socialist countries are able to overcome the present impasse, the crisis in which they found themselves."[29]

The famous "Letter of Six" that Brucan reportedly wrote and passed on to the foreign press through Western diplomats was even more imbued with Communist concepts and language. This style was to be expected, however, from six prominent veterans of the Romanian Communist Party challenging Ceausescu from within the party, a move that attracted great interest both inside and outside Romania.

After the Romanian Revolution, Silviu Brucan shed his Marxist garb and declared communism dead in Romania. When asked about his political leanings during a lecture at the Center for Strategic and International Studies (CSIS) in Washington in the spring of 1990, he described himself as "a radical thinker of the left." In Romania and abroad he was seen in the immediate aftermath of the revolution as the main conservative force in the new leadership, where he served as chairman of its Foreign Policy Commission and as *éminence grise*. It may have been an inaccurate perception. Irrepressibly talkative, he gave lots of interviews and wrote many articles with a characteristic bluntness that irritated many people. When I interviewed him in March 1990, he aggressively defended the new regime, denying all charges regarding its neo-Communist leanings, the threatening presence of the security police, the preservation of the old power and political structures ("You are riding a dead horse," he lashed out at the interviewer) and assailing critics of the National Salvation Front in caustic terms.

Nonetheless, Brucan must have also fought many battles within the National Salvation Front's leadership, from which he was dropped a few months after the revolution. Some observers believe that under his conservative appearance, Brucan may have been a more progressive force than initially thought and, in any case, a more rational voice at a time of great political fluidity. Some of his most controversial utterances, such as his estimate that Romania will need 20 years to reach a fully developed democratic society, have since been accepted at least as a debating point in intellectual circles of the opposition. For the ruling National Salvation Front, of which he remains a part although not a supporter of President Iliescu, he is a force to be reckoned with.

It is unclear how active a participant Brucan was in the conspiracy and how much influence his ideas had in forging a common stand for the group beyond its anti-Ceausescu passions. There may be two indications in this respect. According to General Militaru's testimony, all that the plotters wanted initially was to replace Ceausescu at the head of the party. No thought was given to changing the Communist system itself. Only in recent years was such a change contemplated. "Recent years" may still be an exaggeration, however, knowing the many Marxist idiosyncracies still in evidence with NSF leaders. Militaru also said that Brucan's RFE interview "had defined the program of an alternative to Ceausescu's policy." Although he did not specifically indicate that Brucan's program was the conspiracy's program, the implication was that it must have played a role in the participants' thinking. It was not a program for a change of system, however, but a program heavily influenced by Soviet leader Mikhail Gorbachev's reformist ideas.

The Foreign Connection

One practical task that Brucan could have carried out on behalf of the plotters was to establish contacts with certain foreign powers. A frequent traveler abroad, he was in a position to make the conspiracy known to potential foreign supporters. In 1988, he spent several months in the United States and on his way back home made stops in Britain, Austria, and the Soviet Union. Brucan said he had talks "at the State Department and Foreign Office level" in Washington and London. On my inquiry, U.S. officials admitted that some talks were held, but they insisted the United States did not know about the existence of an organized opposition to Ceausescu, let alone of a conspiracy. British officials had nothing to say regarding Brucan's statement.

In the West, only France has acknowledged having been aware, before the revolution, of a group of party members hostile to Ceausescu, but has not indicated the source of the information. French Foreign Minister Roland Dumas knew, as he explained in a radio interview on January 3, 1990, because the French ambassador to Bucharest "had done his job." He added that the Soviet Union "undoubtedly knew it too."[30]

The Soviets must indeed have known for a rather long time. General Militaru revealed in his *Adevarul* interview that as early as 1984 and perhaps earlier he had approached a Soviet diplomat stationed in Bucharest and the Soviet

consul in Constanta to request the special pistols the conspirators needed for their planned putsch that same year.
"Although these Soviets showed great interest in our plans,"
he said, "the response from Moscow was definitely negative,
barring any interference in Romanian internal affairs by the
Soviet diplomats." Be that as it may, Moscow learned about
the "generals' conspiracy" early on and from a direct source.
"They knew everything," Militaru emphasized. "They also
knew the mood prevailing in the large Romanian enter-
prises, primarily in those producing goods for the Soviet
Union, where engineers, Soviet specialists were present all
the time. Specialists in everything. . . . " When the interviewer observed that "it was curious the Soviets did not
warn Ceausescu" about the conspiracy, Militaru hinted, "It
was not curious."

As noted earlier, Silviu Brucan stopped in Moscow on
his way home from Washington and London in November
1988. After that visit he met privately in Vienna with an
RFE analyst and expressed disappointment that he had
been received "only" by academics and researchers. In his
joint interview with Militaru, however, Brucan disclosed
that he had had talks "at the Kremlin." It is unlikely to have
been a slip of the tongue because the interview was certainly reviewed very carefully before publication, and it is not
the kind of statement an experienced man like Brucan
would make casually. Furthermore, it is significant that he
made that disclosure in August 1990. Almost eight months
earlier, on January 3, 1990, in an interview on the British
Independent Television (ITV) network he stated that while
in Moscow, he received some sort of promise of support in
case of Ceausescu's downfall, albeit "a very reluctant one."[31]

This assertion prompted a reaction from the Soviets.
According to Foreign Ministry spokesman Gennady Gerasi-
mov, "Our research at the Foreign Ministry has led us to the
conclusion that there was no official promise of that sort."
A few days later Foreign Minister Shevardnadze stated in
Bucharest that "there were no contacts" with the new Romanian leaders "before the uprising."[32] At the time of

Shevardnadze's statement, Brucan was still a prominent member of the new Romanian leadership.

There might be some diplomatic subtleties that explain the discrepancy, short of one side's lying. In any case Brucan, while mentioning his talks at the Kremlin in 1988, made it clear that he found there "the same concern to avoid involvement in the internal affairs of Romania." Yet he was regularly visited by Stanislav Petukhov, the Bucharest correspondent of *Pravda*, "thus signaling to the Romanian authorities a Soviet interest in my person."[33]

Brucan's ego may have something to do with his disclosure, but it is unlikely that he would make up a story in such a sensitive area. The fact that he played down for so long his trip to Moscow and the insistence of Soviet denials of any contacts with the anti-Ceausescu conspirators are a bit suspect. They show at the least how concerned the Soviets were about the charges that they were involved in the ousting of Ceausescu.

A Soviet Involvement?

Such charges have been widespread. They were based generally on circumstantial evidence and on suppositions. The arguments most often brought forward by the many proponents of a Soviet involvement included Ceausescu's own suspicions, the Hungarians' role as proxies for Moscow, the alleged pro-Soviet leanings of several of the new Romanian leaders, the Soviet offer of help in the immediate aftermath of the revolution, the Bessarabian issue, and the geopolitical context. All these arguments raise some interesting questions but make less than a convincing case for a theory that would portray the Romanian Revolution as Soviet-guided.

Ceausescu himself seemed genuinely convinced, although apparently in reaction to his gut feeling rather than direct evidence, that the Timisoara demonstrations and their Bucharest follow-up had been orchestrated from abroad. He implicated, however, both the East and the West, with great emphasis on "fascist elements" serving "various foreign interests, espionage services, imperialist, reactionary circles," betraying their homeland "for a handful of dollars or other [hard] currencies" and on "traitors" who attempted to infringe on the country's "territorial integrity" and "to break up Romania."[34] The language Ceausescu used was his usual description of people connected to the West and to Hungary rather than to the Soviet Union. The involvement of a Hungarian clergyman in the initial stages of the unrest and the role played by the Hungarian media as a prime source of information in the first days of the upheaval must have fed his suspicions. Besides, the anti-Hungarian card was one of the few still in his hands to play at that moment.

During his trial, however, Colonel Filip Teodorescu, deputy director of the Counterespionage Directorate, said that he did catch a few spies but would not disclose their nationality or their role in the uprising because of an order to keep his mouth shut. The subject came up in other trials of *Securitate* officers as well. General Iulian Vlad, head of the *Securitate*, insisted that he had indications of an involvement "of a foreign hand" in Timisoara. Testifying in court, he cited "illegal crossing of the Western and South-Western borders by very many people during the weeks preceding the events there." (The western and southwestern neighbors of Romania are Hungary and Yugoslavia.) These people were sent, according to Vlad, with different missions, such as "spreading of written material of a certain character" or "organizing street demonstrations." He also mentioned numerous demands for entry visas from foreign correspondents in the second half of December. Like the others, Vlad produced no evidence to support his claims, such as identification of agents and their country (or countries) of origin, where and how they were apprehended, or what happened to them. He was not asked, and did not volunteer, to respond to the obvious question: If the spies were caught, how did they manage to foment the unrest? Nevertheless, the general emphatically stated that in December "some foreign powers were interested" in generating chaos, and they succeeded. "The country," Vlad added, "was practically opened to all foreign intelligence services and all forms of sabotage and undermining."[35]

None of these statements and allegations is necessarily truthful or reliable. The way they were highlighted and interpreted by some Romanian journalists and publications known for their connections with the *Securitate* makes them very suspect. They form a dubious line of defense for the *Securitate* officers involved in different trials and for the security police as a whole, a defense that tries to suggest that all they did in December was to defend the country against foreign spies and saboteurs. Some ultranationalist groups also embraced the idea of foreign elements stirring up trouble in Timisoara and other cities of Transylvania as proof of a Hungarian interest in destabilizing Romania. Never mind that, if true, the interference resulted in the overthrow of the hideous regime of Ceausescu. They would rather have had no revolution than one even marginally provoked by foreign agents.

In any case, all eyewitness accounts and other testimonies point to entirely improvised, spontaneous, and leaderless protest actions both during the vigil at the Reformed Church and the mass demonstrations in later days. If there was any involvement of foreign agents or incitement of any kind, they must have been too artful and insidious or peripheral to be picked up by witnesses.

As for foreign journalists, there were few if any in Timisoara at the beginning of the unrest. This fact explains why there was so much confusion in the international press about the demonstrations, clashes, and casualties. Virtually all of the information that the international media, including RFE, carried was based on stories from travelers who were either understating or exaggerating the truth. The media was desperately trying to find out what was going on, with meager results. I myself constantly called the U.S. State Department in an attempt to get independent clarification of the conflicting reports from Romania. I was told that as soon as the news of a massacre in Timisoara was heard, two diplomats from the U.S. embassy left Bucharest by car to investigate what happened. They never reached Timisoara, because they were turned back by the police halfway from Bucharest.

Of course, many news organizations wanted to send their correspondents to Romania when word got out that major developments were taking place there. Requests for entry visas from foreign journalists suddenly multiplied in the second half of December, as General Vlad said. There is hardly anything suspect in this. No visa was granted before December 22 anyhow.

There is no indication of foreign involvement in the anti-Ceausescu demonstrations in Bucharest either. It is true that the spontaneity of the very first display of hostility toward Ceausescu during the support rally that the dictator summoned on the morning of December 21 is called into question somewhat by certain circumstances, widely reported but never documented. These reports assert that the shouts and shifting that interrupted Ceausescu's speech were preceded or accompanied (the reports conflict) by some sort of firecrackers set off among the crowd. Aside from the firecrackers, some accounts claim that the sound of shooting or of moving tanks was played in the square, apparently over the loudspeakers that were set up to enthuse the crowd with prerecorded cheers for the leader.[36] Reportedly the objective was to create panic and disturb the rally. Another version contends, however, that the firecrackers were meant as a signal for the beginning of the anti-Ceausescu demonstration. Other stories and interpretations were put forward as well. In any case, if there is anything to these reports, they would tend to indicate a certain amount of premeditation with complicity from within the power structure rather than from foreign agents. Later on, though, the demonstrations seem to have been purely spontaneous. On the other hand, the coup itself, if there was one, was anything but spontaneous and therefore the opportunities for foreign interference were much greater there.

The alleged pro-Soviet inclinations of some of the conspirators and new Romanian leaders are highlighted widely in articles and books. West German analyst Anneli Ute Gabanyi even talks of a whole "internationalist faction represented by suppressed functionaries [Silviu Brucan] or by their sons [Iliescu, Roman]" who, after almost 30 years, grabbed power again in the party and state.[37] Whether an "internationalist faction" has ever existed as such in the Romanian Communist Party is an open question. There was virtually no resistance to the more autonomous line espoused by the Romanian party under Gheorghe Gheorghiu-Dej in 1964 and continued under Ceausescu; all the "internationalists" joined, for better or worse, the "nationalist" faction.

Generally, any pro-Soviet leanings are hard to prove. There might be a strong case regarding General Militaru, if it is true that he was a Soviet spy in the 1970s. Former Intelligence Chief Ion Mihai Pacepa firmly stands by his story as told in his book.[38] Militaru's denial aside, it may be difficult to distinguish between his anti-Ceausescu passions and his alleged Soviet connection. (One of the conspirators once said that they would have entered into a pact with the Devil himself had that led to the ouster of Ceausescu.)

Regarding Iliescu, if there is any pro-Soviet bias it has nothing to do with his father, who did not play much of a role in the party. Analysts focused their interest on his years spent in Moscow as a student in the 1950s. Some news stories reported that during those years he met and even socialized with Gorbachev, who attended Moscow University at the same time. Although such a possibility should not be discounted, no evidence was presented, and the two categorically have denied it. In his RFE interview, Iliescu wondered who it was that spread this rumor—his friends or Ceausescu's agents. Even if the rumor were true, it would be extremely speculative to view it either as a basis for collusion or as evidence of political preferences.

As soon as Ceausescu fled, however, it seems that one of Iliescu's absolute priorities was to get in touch with the Soviets. During the meeting that created the National Salvation Front, a suggestion was made that the front should make known to the world that "we are maintaining our alliances and don't change [our] international commitments." Iliescu said, "I want to tell you that I got in touch with the Soviet Embassy and I already let them know the situation in which we find ourselves in order that they convey to Moscow for them to know who we are and what we want. This I already told them."[39]

In what capacity and on whose behalf did he make that call? He had no official position at the time; the National Salvation Front was not yet in existence; no government exercised power. The "we" supposedly gathered for the first time during that meeting to form a governing body to fill the vacuum of power left by Ceausescu's flight. The incident is strange and suspect. It fed the suspicions of a coup. Yet it proves nothing in terms of a Soviet involvement. If anything, it suggests that the Soviets may have been in the dark about "who they were and what they wanted," if they needed to be told. A transcript of that conversation between Iliescu and whoever it was at the Soviet Embassy may be instructive anyhow.

There were also reports about Iliescu and perhaps other leaders visiting the Soviet Embassy during their first or second day in power. One such report is contained in Dumitru Mazilu's memoirs. Describing the first night of the new leadership at the television station, the former number two writes that early next morning a decision was made to move to another place. As he was entering an armored personnel carrier, another vehicle was just leaving in front of him, supposedly carrying Iliescu and some of the others. The driver wanted to take Mazilu to the Soviet Embassy, where, he said, the others went. The vice president decided, according to his memoirs, that "it was not acceptable" to go there and instructed his driver to take him instead to the Central Committee building.[40]

Besides Iliescu, others among the initial group of people in authority were said to have studied in Moscow. This biographical detail may or may not be significant. Still others, including influential members of the postrevolutionary governments, had studied in the West. That does not necessarily make them proponents of capitalism. Ceausescu himself had studied in Moscow (Russian being the only foreign language that he somewhat understood), but that did not turn him into a pro-Russian.

No Taste for Intervention

As for the Soviet offer of military assistance during the fighting that followed Ceausescu's downfall, it was at least peculiar. The only known offer came during the so-called night of the generals, the first night of fighting. (It was called this because a camera recorded the flurry of activity in the room that served as command post for operations against the terrorists, where General Stefan Guse, chief of staff of the Romanian Army, and General Iulian Vlad, head of the *Securitate*, established their makeshift headquarters. The videocassette was shown later on Romanian television, and I carefully watched a copy.) At a certain point, General Guse took a call from somebody who spoke Russian. He did not understand what was being said and was shown passing the phone to an interpreter. On the phone was a representative of the Soviet Embassy in Bucharest offering military assistance. Guse nervously rejected it, saying that the Romanian forces could deal with the situation alone.

It appears that the new political leadership did not share General Guse's assessment of the situation or his nervousness about Soviet intervention. The new leaders seem to have wanted help from the Soviets and asked for it. There is some controversy, however, with most of the main players denying they ever requested Soviet intervention. Yet, one of them – then First Vice Chairman Dumitru Mazilu – asserts in his already cited memoirs (written in Switzerland and published in a New York Romanian newspaper) that President Iliescu "insisted on accepting 'the Soviet assistance in order to stop the armed resistance.' Moreover," Mazilu adds, "certain of obtaining the agreement from us, the other leaders of the new power, he had [already] presented the Soviet leadership with an official request of help, which they [the Soviets], after some hesitation, were inclined to provide."[41] According to Mazilu, this request explains why the Soviets had already prepared helicopters and had informed the Romanian Army stationed in Moldavia, at the border with the Soviet Union, of their intention to fly them over Romanian territory toward Bucharest *at the request of the National Salvation Front's command.*" This account confirms General Guse's strong opposition to any Soviet involvement and maintains that it was decisive in avoiding Soviet intervention.[42] In any case, on December 23, 1989, between 10:00 and 11:00 A.M., Romanian television and Radio Bucharest in a joint broadcast carried the following announcement: "We are informed that the help of the Soviet army was requested through the Embassy of the USSR, due to the fact that the terrorists have resorted to helicopters through foreign interventionists."

Mikhail Gorbachev himself confirmed later that same day that appeals for Soviet help were made by the Romanian National Salvation Front Council "in connection with the fact that a number of sub-units came out against the people." Speaking in the Congress of the People's Deputies, the Soviet leader said, however, that in the meantime the situation had become "less acute" and the Romanian chief of staff "has stated confidently that the whole situation is under control." All Gorbachev offered to send to Romania was humanitarian aid for the wounded, in coordination with the other Warsaw Pact countries. Prime Minister Nikolai Ryzhkov was more specific, excluding military aid as "inadmissible," but offering other aid "such as medical or food aid" deemed necessary "to support the changes occurring there."[43] Gorbachev brought up the issue again the next day by informing the People's Congress that the National Salvation Front had asked Moscow to replenish the Romanian Army's ammunition supplies. He alluded once more to General Guse's statement (apparently the response he gave to the call from the Soviet Embassy during the night of December 22–23) that the army was in control and needed no help as an explanation of why the Soviet Union was not contemplating direct intervention in Romania.

According to Captain Mihai Lupoi, a founding member of the front and minister of tourism in the first postrevolutionary government, the Soviets flatly turned down the Romanian request for intervention. Lupoi, who fell out with the National Salvation Front and asked for political asylum in Switzerland in July 1990, added that all that Moscow promised was to meet the Romanian Army's needs for ammunition.[44]

The Soviet restraint is remarkable and uncharacteristic, especially given that Moscow had, in addition to the apparent request of the Romanian leadership, what amounted to a public blessing from two major Western powers.

It should be remembered that the apparent resistance by pro-Ceausescu forces to the new regime worried many governments. At that time, the new regime received the enthusiastic support of all Western nations. On December 24, 1989, French Foreign Minister Dumas offered to help organize a brigade of volunteers for Romania. At the same time, he stated that if the Soviet Union decided to intervene, France "not only would not object to it, but would support this action."[45] The same day, U.S. Secretary of State James A. Baker was asked on NBC TV's "Meet the Press" about a possible Soviet intervention in Romania. He responded, "We would be inclined probably to follow the example of France, who has said that if the Warsaw Pact felt necessary to intervene on behalf of the opposition, that it would support that action."[46] Although this statement surprised many observers and was strongly criticized by some conservative experts, it must have sounded encouraging in Moscow. The State Department later distanced itself from the statement and in fact repudiated it. A knowledgeable State Department official told me months later in a personal interview that Secretary Baker, who had just returned from a vacation in Texas, improvised his answer without having consulted anybody in the department.

Whatever the Soviet reasoning, no armed intervention did occur, and the danger posed by the terrorists turned out to be greatly exaggerated at the time. This area is murky, however, and requires more clarification from all parties involved before it can be known exactly what happened.

The Bessarabian Issue

At the time there were some rumors that special units of Bessarabians were being formed to be sent to Romania in case of a Soviet intervention. Bessarabians are Romanians who live on a piece of land that was part of prewar Romania but was annexed by the Soviet Union under the infamous Molotov-Ribbentrop pact of 1939. Part of what was previously called Bessarabia became Soviet Moldavia. Although this annexation was always a sensitive issue between the Soviet Union and Romania, for 45 years of Communist rule it was generally kept out of public controversy.

Some analysts contended that the Bessarabian issue must have been high on the Soviets' list of motives to support or even foment an anti-Ceausescu putsch. The reasoning was that the Soviets would have been inclined to favor "internationalists," pro-Soviet elements in the Romanian Communist Party who were unlikely to raise the question of Bessarabia. The question was raised, however, not by Romania, but by the inhabitants of the territory themselves. The majority of them are Romanians, and a strong movement of national and political emancipation developed during 1989. Interestingly enough, "nationalist" Ceausescu had paid little public attention to that movement, and the bleak situation in Romania under Ceausescu was anything but attractive to the Bessarabians.[47] Moscow could not hope for a better set of circumstances.

Moscow's satisfaction could be detected in the way the Soviet press treated Ceausescu's Romania and in the very sustained pace of bilateral economic cooperation. At a time when most of the international press, both in the West and in the East, was sharply critical of the disastrous Romanian situation, the Soviet media remained generally silent, with very few exceptions. It seemed as though *glasnost* was being applied to all subjects except Romania.[48] Moscow and Bucharest gave the impression that they were following a kind of gentlemen's agreement whereby the latter kept quiet on Bessarabia and the former did the same thing on the situation in Romania. The Soviets broke that quid pro quo a couple of times, and Ceausescu retorted by obliquely raising the Bessarabian issue in his speech at the 14th Party Congress in November 1989. Nonetheless, the apparent arrangement remained basically in place until the revolution.

One can argue that Moscow was better off with Ceausescu as far as Bessarabia was concerned: He could be kept in line with economic incentives and political pressure, and, most of all, his Romania was no magnet. After the revolution, with supposedly friendly people in government in Bucharest, the Bessarabian issue is much more of an annoyance to Moscow. The exchanges between Soviet Moldavia and Romania have been much accelerated; the border has been opened; and the chances of returning the territory to Romania are discussed openly on both sides of the Prut.

It is not a question of the purity of Soviet goals toward Romania. Hardly any other nation has suffered more under Soviet domination and under the communism brought to Romania by Soviet tanks. Quite possibly the future could reveal that Moscow did have a more active role in the developments that led to Ceausescu's demise. All that can be noted now, however great one's innate suspicions, is that the evidence does not point to a major Soviet involvement. Moscow lost the cold war and retreated from Central and

Eastern Europe. Why would the Soviets care more about Romania than they cared about such countries of vital strategic importance as East Germany, Poland, Czechoslovakia, or even Hungary, where they had much more leverage, including troops, to influence the situation?

Over the years, Romania's strategic significance fluctuated for the Soviet Union. The Soviets withdrew their troops from Romania back in the 1950s, at the height of the cold war.[49] Then they tolerated Ceausescu's independence game for a quarter of a century, while crushing attempts at autonomy in other satellite countries. Gorbachev had not shown much eagerness to take a stand for reforms in Romania or against Ceausescu. He made some waves during a state visit to Bucharest in 1988 by obliquely criticizing the Romanian regime with some negative remarks about nepotism. On the Romanian dictator's 70th birthday, however, Gorbachev even awarded him the highest Soviet decoration—the Order of Lenin—less than two years before the revolution. The Soviet stance was noticed with some amazement in the West. I remember a story that I heard from a Western diplomat in early July 1989 while I was in Paris to cover the Helsinki follow-up conference. It was about an exchange between my interlocutor and a Soviet diplomat in which the Westerner inquired about Moscow's inaction and apparent indifference towards Romania. "Why don't you support reform in Romania as well?" he asked. "Do you know any reformist in Romania?" came the Soviet's shrewd reply.

There are those who invoke Malta as a kind of new Yalta—that is, a new U.S.–Soviet arrangement that would leave certain countries, namely Romania and Bulgaria, in a Soviet zone of influence. The absurdity of such a suggestion is apparent. U.S. officials simply ridicule these charges. Even if "the Malta sell-out" had occurred, why would Romania have to remain behind Bulgaria and behind the Soviet Union itself in the democratization process? This scenario does not make any sense either as a debating argument or as an excuse.

A Balance Sheet: One Revolution, Many Plotters

There is little doubt that small groups of former officials and high-ranking officers conspired on and off over many years to topple Ceausescu. Nothing suggests they ever had a chance of succeeding. The only time when they actually devised a plan of action was in 1984, and they failed miserably even before trying. This statement is not to deny the courage and the dedication of the people involved, but to put things in perspective. In any case, there is no indication whatsoever that they intended anything other than removing Ceausescu from power and replacing him with a leader more attuned to the times. After all, they were themselves Communists. Besides, the times were different. During the dark era of Ceausescu's rule, a more liberal kind of socialism looked definitely like a desirable improvement. In the 1970s and most of the 1980s, the geopolitical environment was not conducive to a radical systemic change and many "realists," both in the East and in the West, sought to limit their horizons voluntarily and to accept mild reformism and then Gorbachevism, at least as an intermediate goal.

Then, however, history accelerated its pace all over Eastern and Central Europe. Communism lost any chance of survival. The Communists ran for cover, hurriedly converting into Socialists or Social Democrats. In most countries they put up little resistance to change. The process was peaceful and gradual.

The process was neither peaceful nor gradual in Romania, however. As Michael Shafir puts it,

> In the other countries of the Warsaw Pact, political change has either been preceded by a long period of incubation, during which important segments of society had time to work out possible alternatives to the existing regimes [Poland, Hungary, and Czechoslovakia], or had at least come about against the background of unmistakable signs of Soviet encouragement of an alternative to the existing leadership of the ruling party [East Germany and Bulgaria]. Neither of these

factors facilitating a relatively peaceful transfer of power existed in Romania.[50]

In Romania, change was sudden and violent.

It is interesting to note the conspirators' claim that they hoped to launch their coup in the spring of 1990 and subsequently to stir a popular revolt to neutralize any lingering resistance from the Ceausescu forces. Instead, in a complete reversal of roles, the people started the revolution and sustained it for several days, with substantial human sacrifices. The benefits of power reverted to the plotters, however. They simply climbed the crest of the revolutionary wave.

They argue they deserved it because the popular uprising could succeed only as a result of a massive change of heart within the army and *Securitate*. It is indeed fairly obvious that the revolution was successful because of certain actions and, more important, *inaction* within the regime's power structure. Many parts of the army and *Securitate* definitely deserted Ceausescu and refused to defend his regime in the face of a determined popular revolt (which is not to say they were on the side of revolution). What is not so obvious is that this was the plotters' doing. There are many reasons for skepticism. For one thing, the information is still very limited. Many details are being withheld.[51] The actors known now may not have been as effective as they claim to have been. Most of those named do not seem to have been involved in any effective action in the days before Ceausescu's ouster, while some of those instrumental in the dictator's fall were not involved in the plot. Iliescu, for example, was not in regular communication with the alleged conspirators since Militaru could not get in touch with him other than by a television broadcast.[52] Brucan was under house arrest on the outskirts of Bucharest and, according to his own account, learned from a neighbor about Ceausescu's flight. He and Militaru did not know each other personally.[53]

On the other hand, Ceausescu's defense minister Vasile

Milea, who actually ordered the army to stop shooting at the demonstrators, was not part of the conspiracy, as Militaru pointed out. Furthermore, one of the first measures taken by Militaru as defense minister was to call back from retirement a number of generals, supposedly his coconspirators, an indication that the new regime did not quite trust the team of generals in place. The 20 generals who, according to Militaru and Brucan, were part of the conspiracy were mostly in retirement.

Because of such circumstances, the revelations raise more questions than they answered. At the most, what the conspirators may have done was to make full use of the popular uprising to ease Ceausescu out and replace him with their own people with as little trouble as possible. The army and *Securitate* may have switched sides on their own, independent of the conspiracy, and only after being confronted with a popular revolution.

Therefore, perhaps a likelier scenario could be described as follows: with the vigil at the Reformed Church in Timisoara expanding to a full-scale, anti-Ceausescu uprising, it became clear that this time was the real thing. Faced with a revolutionary and bloody situation, some people in the army and the *Securitate* became hesitant. First they tried cleverly to avoid carrying out Ceausescu's orders. Then, when the dictator became aggressive and accused several of the top army and *Securitate* leaders of treason, threatening to court-martial them, they turned against him. During the seven days of the revolution, a sort of slow realization of the imminent fall of the regime took hold among many of the officers. On the night of December 21 and the morning of December 22, the shift was completed. Some of the conspirators and Iliescu in particular may have struck a deal with the commanders of the army and *Securitate* troops, but not before the revolution started. The deal was probably struck, directly or by proxies, while the revolution was unfolding and expanding. Then different groups and individuals within the power structure looking for a way out of the crisis came together and staged what can be called a collective coup. What did President Iliescu say? He said: "We may just as well speak of several conspiracies."[54]

If this scenario is what happened, it is clear that the spontaneous popular revolution is what brought down the dictatorship. It forced large parts of the power structure first to blink and then to search for ways to save themselves. When this search began, the group of conspirators got their chance, and they seized it swiftly and anxiously. In short, they did not make the revolution. It was the people, the revolutionaries, spearheaded by the youth, who fought the bloody battles. The conspirators, practically all of them, just reaped the fruits – at least for a while. After all, Iliescu and his chief of intelligence are the only ones of the named conspirators still in power. All the others are on the sidelines.

The question of the nature of change would dominate the battle of ideas as well as the political convulsions of postrevolutionary Romania. Was it just an anti-Ceausescu uprising or an anti-Communist one? What did it set out to accomplish – a change of personnel or a systemic mutation? Was its goal to "humanize" socialism or institute Western-style democracy? Did it intend to patch up the state-controlled economy or convert it into a free market economy? The answers would be clouded by suspicion, by political immaturity, by half-truths and outright lies, by vacillation and inhibition, and perhaps most of all by an obsession with power.

5

Purgatory

Romanian writer and essayist Octavian Paler perceptively noted that it is not easy to achieve normality when you just left hell. A purgatory is needed, a stage of purification. Although nobody contests that Romania emerged from hell at the end of December 1989, few profess to know what exactly purgatory means in this particular case and whether it really leads to paradise. The only certainty is that it implies pain, and there was lots of it in the aftermath of the December revolution. Most of it was a result of the dire consequences of more than 40 years of Communist rule, but some of it was self-inflicted. The political, economic, social, moral, spiritual, and psychological readjustment has been more traumatic in Romania than in other Eastern and Central European nations. The reasons are numerous. For one thing, the Ceausescu dictatorship was uncommonly harsh, whimsical, intruding, manipulative, and corrupt, leaving deep scars on the people and on society. In addition, the leaders who took power after the uprising were apparently unaware of the depth of the crisis and ill-equipped to deal with it.

The Original Sin

From the very beginning, the new rulers had to face what Romanian writer Ion Buduca called "the original sin" – that

120

is, the questionable legitimacy of their power. Legitimacy is an issue that has always troubled every totalitarian regime. What Romania had, however, was a supposedly revolutionary order that had issued from a popular uprising facing a similar legitimacy problem and being haunted by it. It should not have been too surprising because it stemmed from the striking paradox of a basically anti-Communist revolution producing a regime dominated by former Communists. Ion Iliescu and most of the others who formed the inner circle that took power in the wake of the uprising were former members of the Romanian Communist Party, as were, with two or three exceptions, the new ministers. It is true that some of the most prominent new leaders opposed Ceausescu. They even ordered him killed. Besides, being a former Communist would not necessarily preclude a conversion to democratic convictions, as happened many a time in the past, mostly in the West.[1] The question was, were these people real converts to democracy; did they free themselves of their Communist background? The answer was at best ambiguous.

In Iliescu's case, the apprehension was heightened by the fact that he had been not just an ordinary member of the party, but one of its leading activists, first as head of the youth organization, then as a Central Committee secretary for propaganda, and as a candidate member of the ruling Political Executive Committee even after his advertised break with Ceausescu and until 1984. During the first hours following Ceausescu's flight, he seemed quite imbued by the Communist imagery and manner of speaking. When he spoke in front of the cameras or in private meetings, for example, he invariably used the appellation "comrade," and people addressed him with the same word. During one of his televised speeches on December 22, 1989, he seemed to try to dissociate the Communist Party and communism from the Ceausescu dictatorship. He said that the previous leaders "proclaimed themselves communists." "They have nothing to do either with socialism or with the ideology of scientific communism," Iliescu said. "They have only defiled the

name of the Romanian Communist Party, they have only
defiled the memory of those who have sacrificed their lives
for the cause of socialism in this country."[2] It is unclear
whether Iliescu had just misspoken or intended to excuse
the party and communism in order to keep them alive. In
any case, the words chosen clearly reflected a state of mind
that was hardly in tune with the meaning of the revolution.

Later, the new leader would adjust his manner of speaking and vocabulary to the changed environment, but there
would still be many indications of Iliescu's inability to free
himself of Communist categories and proclivities. His credibility as a convert to democracy would be often sapped by
his statements and thinking, but most of all by his acts and
behavior. Nevertheless, he would strongly defend himself
by portraying his 1971 quarrel with Ceausescu as a major
political rift. By summer of 1990, that incident became
much more than a break with the dictator; it was presented
as the beginning of a separation from communism as well.
In his interview with the noted literary critic Nicolae Mano-
lescu of *Romania Literara*, in response to a question regarding his views on communism, Iliescu said: "This dissociation [from communism] I accomplished long ago, the
process having clearly started as early as 1971, when I had
the revelation of the failure of communism as an ideology. I
don't think it would be possible to reform communism or
else to create a kind of communism with a human face. For
me, this issue is an ideological fact definitively quashed
long ago."[3] Some knowledgeable people seem to doubt at
least the dating of Iliescu's "dissociation." One of them is
General Nicolae Militaru, his alleged coconspirator and
first defense minister, who in his joint interview with Silviu
Brucan published in August 1990 by the newspaper
Adevarul, suggested that as late as 1984, when the plotters
prepared a coup against Ceausescu, they were reluctant to
involve Iliescu because they observed "a reticence on his
part for any action outside the system."

In any case, the assertion the president made in the
cited interview, coming less than a month after a most seri-

ous breach of democratic and, in fact, civilized behavior—
namely the miners' punitive expedition in Bucharest—was
anything but convincing. At the time of this writing, its
sincerity is yet to be proven.

Iliescu, as noted before, was not alone among the new
leaders with a notorious Communist past. Others, while not
personally identified as leading figures or propagandists of
the party, were strongly connected to the former nomenklatura by family ties or otherwise. Petre Roman, the 44-year-
old university professor who became prime minster of the
new government, is the son of a prominent Communist,
Valter Roman, a veteran of the Spanish War and an activist
of the Comintern in Moscow and elsewhere. The elder Roman, who died in 1983, never reached the highest echelon in
the party hierarchy, the Politburo, but as a leading Communist intellectual, influential and well-connected, for many
years directed the publishing house for political writings.
He also played an important role in the army after the Communist takeover, rising to the rank of general. His son, although a member of the party, was not politically active,
following instead a successful academic career. He studied
power engineering in Romania and spent three years as a
graduate student in Toulouse, France. He taught at the
Bucharest Polytechnical Institute for almost two decades
before becoming Romania's prime minster in the wake of
the revolution, in which he seems to have been an active
participant with a group of his students. Although this
participation is supposed to have brought him to the leadership of the National Salvation Front, it is much likelier that
his connection to Iliescu was what really counted in his
being assigned the premiership. (Although there is no proof
of his being a part of any conspiracy, some sources speculate that this connection may explain his presence among
the anti-Ceausescu demonstrators.)

Most of the ministers in Roman's first government were
high officials of the previous administration from the second or third ranks, as were virtually all local officials; they
hardly represented a break with the just overthrown regime.

In general, any harsh criticism was carefully channeled toward the Ceausescus and their cronies and away from the Communist system itself. No one was tried for crimes committed over the decades of Communist rule, for the economic disaster, for the killings in jails and detention camps, or for the calamitous policies in virtually every field of human endeavor. Certain charges were mentioned during the Ceausescus' trial, but never during his underlings' prosecution. Those few who were brought to trial were charged invariably with genocide or complicity in genocide – in fact, for their approval of Ceausescu's decision to fire on the demonstrators. The new leaders never initiated a full-scale critical analysis of the 40 years of communism, and when the opposition attempted to do so, it was accused of "witch hunting."

The new regime pretended to be the authentic emanation of the revolution and would not share power with anybody. It even delayed the normal separation of powers that any democracy, no matter how imperfect, implements, until it was forced to do so by demonstrations and unrest. The claim to legitimacy by virtue of the very genuineness of the popular uprising was rather shaky and caught the new power in a serious dilemma: On the one hand, by its leaders' own initial admission, with Roman's possible exception, they were not active participants in the uprising; therefore, how could they be its mouthpiece? On the other hand, they would not admit they took part in a conspiracy to topple Ceausescu (as some of them did admit later, when no longer in power) for fear of being seen as beneficiaries of a palace putsch rather than as products of widespread discontent and desire for change. Moreover, their illegitimacy was loudly proclaimed by many revolutionaries, former dissidents, and organizations.

As a remedy, the National Salvation Front sought to organize general elections at the earliest date possible. Two additional problems arose: First, early elections (the initial proposal was for March) were strongly opposed by the opposition parties that were just taking shape and lacked everything from typewriters, telephones, and office furniture to an organizational framework, experienced leadership, or means to get their word to the people around the country. Second, how would the power itself be represented in the election? After much behind-the-scenes bickering, public polemics, and street confrontations, an agreement was reached for elections to be held on May 20, 1990, and a kind of mini-parliament to be formed with all the parties (more than 30 at that date) represented. This mini-parliament was in many respects a parody of any real representative democracy, but it embodied at least a certain separation of powers and a limited sharing of authority. Its main piece of legislation was the electoral law, which included, besides detailed provisions for the development of the electoral process, some elements of constitutional order. A modicum of cohesion was achieved among the parties, but legitimacy was not at hand. The primary reasons for lack of legitimacy were still there, and at least one more, of major significance, had been added.

That significant addition was the National Salvation Front's decision to run as the governing body in the election, in spite of its explicit commitment to avoid exactly that. For many analysts, this decision launched the first major political crisis of postrevolutionary Romania. The front constituted itself as the new power that filled the vacuum left by the collapse of Ceausescu's regime—legislating, governing the country, and indirectly administering justice. It was not a political movement and stated clearly its determination not to become one. One month later, however, the leadership of the front changed its mind. Power itself became a contestant in the election—blurring, in fact erasing, the boundary between player and referee and bursting into the political arena with an overwhelming advantage.

The question was not whether Iliescu, Roman, Brucan, or anybody else had a right to run in elections, but how they did it. Had they formed their own party few would have objected. By bringing the front itself into the electoral contest they resurrected the old Communist hegemonic ambition. Moreover, this decision was presented as an original concept of democracy in which pluralism may not necessarily mean different parties, the National Salvation Front being a politically and philosophically heterogeneous movement and a kind of umbrella organization. Many saw in this promotion of an "original" model a rejection of Western democracy. Prominent Romanian philosopher Gabriel Liiceanu put it in these words:

> Original democracy presupposes a different type of democracy than democracy. Democracy is democracy. Democratic democracy. It is the classical European democracy. Let's name it: it's Western type democracy. There is no better one. . . . We have a need now for old things, not for new things. Not for experiments. These are very dangerous.[4]

The resounding victory of the front and of Iliescu in the election alleviated the legitimacy problem but did not eliminate it altogether because of several factors, including some linked to the electoral process and more important to developments that bordered on sheer lawlessness.

The Obsession of Power

A state of insecurity and precariousness, perhaps caused and certainly compounded by the deficit of legitimacy, was always evident among the new rulers. More often than not, they behaved erratically, fearful of imaginary coups and subversion, highly suspicious of every anti-Communist or anti-government demonstration, constantly on guard against supposed interference from abroad. It was a kind of inherited or induced paranoia that must have been related to the fragility of the informal and unholy arrangement that put them in power, to their Communist upbringing, and to their long conspiratorial pursuits. Their absolute priority, however, was their wish to maintain the power they gained on December 22. They made deals they probably regretted, offered benefits that came back to haunt them, concluded alliances that tied their hands or retarded their reforms, and allowed or even encouraged provocative distractions or insidious attacks, all to one end – to retain, defend, expand, and strengthen their grip on power.

With the police and the army seriously stung by their role in the repression of the revolution and consequently reluctant to involve themselves in clashes with the opponents of the new regime, the uncertainty and insecurity of the rulers were magnified. Unable to accept opposition as a necessary and beneficial fact of life, scared by every demonstration and haunted by barely concealed fears of a military coup, the rulers were led by their Communist background to rely on the industrial workers, a part of the population that was itself frightened by uncertainties about the future and in need of protection. They promised to go slow on economic reforms, were fuzzy about privatization, approved selective pay raises, and spearheaded a demagogic campaign against foreign capital investment with the slogan "We won't sell our country." To motivate the workers, government leaders went so far as to pit them against intellectuals and students among whom the opposition had more appeal. In spite of everything, however, not all the workers were willing to engage in this dangerous game. Moreover, with new independent trade unions not quite eager to serve as watchdogs and repressive forces of the government, clearly many workers were not considered reliable. The rulers settled, therefore, for that segment of the working class at the same time more vulnerable, less sophisticated, and most privileged in terms of pay and benefits – the miners. Miners would become a kind of private army of thugs, ready for deployment on short notice. They were used twice with disastrous results.

One crucial distinction that Romania gained among the former Communist countries was the willingness of the new leaders to repress the political opposition and to do it with bands of civilians serving at the provisional president's pleasure as surrogate forces of order. Answering his critics, Iliescu often likened the bands of miners to posses in the United States. The Posse Comitatus, however, was a strictly regulated legal right that enabled the sheriff to summon private citizens to assist in maintaining public order; no law in Romania gives such a right to the president of the country. Furthermore, Iliescu strongly denied that he summoned the miners to Bucharest. In historical parallels, perhaps the miners' operation is more reminiscent of the fascist storm troops. Ironically, the president asked for help from the population and subsequently justified the action by alleging on each occasion that the government was facing a "fascist putsch." He repeatedly blamed the Legionnaires, members of the prewar fascist Legion of the Archangel Michael, better known in the West as the Iron Guard. No evidence was ever presented to prove this allegation.

The Pressure of the Street

The first serious political challenge to the new power came a few weeks after the revolution, on January 12, 1990, when several thousand people demonstrated in Victory Square, in front of the massive building that was the headquarters of the provisional government. They loudly expressed their anti-Communist sentiments and their opposition to a regime dominated by Communists. Alarmed and bewildered, the new leaders joined the crowd and complied with its demands. They promised to outlaw immediately the Communist Party and reintroduce the death penalty, abolished after the Ceausescus' execution. The next day, however, they changed their minds and offered to let a popular referendum decide the two measures. After one more day they reneged on their promises altogether. True, the issues were of dubious importance; the party had ceased to exist anyhow, and capital punishment, which was not needed, would have been perhaps even detrimental to social calm. Indeed, organizing a referendum in the extreme uncertainty prevailing at the time was at least impractical, if not hazardous. Still, the behavior of the rulers, including Iliescu and Mazilu, gave rise to doubts regarding their wisdom, competence, steadiness, and reliability.

The main political casualty of that first street confrontation was Dumitru Mazilu, who had served as number two in the top leadership. He was dropped or resigned (depending on whose version one believes) shortly afterward. He later became an opponent of the National Salvation Front and of Iliescu.[5] A prominent dissident in the last years of the Ceausescu dictatorship, Mazilu was said to have been the most determined advocate of a genuine democratization within the new power and a resolute foe of the *Securitate*. Paradoxically, he himself had been a *Securitate* colonel, teaching at its Baneasa school and serving undercover at the United Nations (UN). He turned into an opponent of Ceausescu, however, and as a UN official assigned to write a report on Youth and Human Rights (consequent to a Romanian initiative), set out to denounce the Romanian dictatorship. Prevented by the authorities from leaving Romania and held incommunicado at his home in Bucharest, Mazilu managed to send abroad several letters of protest (some to RFE for broadcast) and the report on Youth and Human Rights itself, a caustic indictment of Ceausescu's tyranny. It was issued as a UN document and had a considerable impact both in Romania (where it became known through RFE) and internationally. A forceful public speaker but prone to high-pitched demagoguery and emotional outbursts, Mazilu had in the immediate aftermath of the revolution a large following that he later lost, mostly for being denounced as a former officer of *Securitate* by *Romania Libera*, the largest independent newspaper. Disparaged, threatened, accused of being a CIA agent, he left the country and settled in Switzerland, where he compiled a critical report on the mid-June 1990 violent events in Bucharest. In March 1991, he was attacked by two Romanian-speaking men in his Geneva home and hospitalized as a result of the assault, which Mazilu and others attributed to the new Romanian security services. His rise and fall illustrate the paradoxes and political zigzagging of the postrevolutionary period.

It is hard to assess whether Mazilu's departure had any impact on the National Salvation Front's policy. From that point on, however, the power certainly dealt differently with demonstrations, giving way to violent intolerance, confrontation, divisive tactics, and a sort of class struggle that would create an environment of severe political and social strain. On January 28, tens of thousands of antigovernment demonstrators once more gathered in Victory Square, this time to protest the National Salvation Front's decision to compete in the forthcoming election, in addition to previous demands that the *Securitate* be dismantled and the government resign.

The new regime was not prepared for a dialogue, let alone concessions. Instead, claiming to be in great danger of being toppled by a coup d'état, it asked for help from the workers. It did not take long for large groups of factory workers to show up, incited by former Communist Party organizers and supporters of the front. The nasty slogan "We work; we don't think" made its appearance. It would become emblematic of the rift between workers and intellectuals, including students, a rift that the National Salvation Front erroneously encouraged for transient political benefits. A counterdemonstration was organized, followed by the ransacking of the opposition parties' headquarters. Some opposition leaders were "saved" by the army. The prime minister himself showed up at the National Peasants' Party, one of the major opposition parties, to pull its leader out of the attacked headquarters and take him to safety in a tank. All street demonstrations were banned, with public gatherings allowed in certain parks and only by prior permit.

After the violent exploits of its supporters, the government thought to move quickly to ease the tension by reaching an agreement with the opposition for the creation of a Provisional Council of National Unity in which all parties would share in governing the country until general elections. While giving each party three seats in this mini-parliament, the arrangement still ensured the National Salvation Front a working majority through several puppet parties hurriedly manufactured and through nonparty personalities who could become members of the new body in their own right. The government may have counted on a certain stability and calm, but nothing of the sort happened; on the contrary, owing primarily to its grave mistakes, the most serious disturbances were still to come.

On February 18, another demonstration took place in Victory Square. It was a beautiful Sunday, and the square was filled by a huge cheerful crowd. Around noon, as the people chanted antigovernment slogans, a group of youngsters suddenly surged forward and started to smash windows and force the main entrance gate of the government building. The soldiers and policemen guarding the building made no attempt to stop them, even when brutalized by the aggressors. Some in the crowd approved of the attack; others chanted "No violence!" For many hours, the doors remained open, and hundreds of people got into the building, mostly from curiosity. They manhandled a deputy prime minister, trying to force him to speak to the crowd. Foreign press correspondents also entered the building, taking photographs or interviewing demonstrators. It was already late at night when the police finally intervened to vacate the government headquarters of the few demonstrators who lingered there. Who were those who started the violence? Most of them were never identified. The opposition and the independent press contended it was all a provocation either by disgruntled security officers or by the government itself.

The Miners Are Coming

The regime reacted with great urgency. Iliescu went on radio and television to warn that Romania may become "a new Lebanon." Overstating the danger, he again appealed for help from the population. This time, however, throngs of miners came by chartered trains and buses to Bucharest from the Jiu Valley, and the consequences of their widespread violence would reverberate for many months. They arrived the day after the Victory Square unrest and were greeted by President Iliescu, who told them that their support "will give the necessary response to the irresponsible elements who carried out yesterday's violence" seeking to "undermine stability, create havoc and make Romania ungovernable." The miners responded: "Down with the hooligans!" and "Iliescu, don't go!" In the wake of this friendly meeting, carried live on Romanian television (in stark contrast to the scant and highly biased coverage of the antigovernment demonstration), the miners went to work, beating people, ransacking offices, and intimidating the opposition, although all the parties represented in the mini-parliament, as well as many organizations, unequivocally condemned the attack on the government headquarters.

The miners' aggression was a kind of dress rehearsal for the much more brutal and consequential foray of the miners in June of the same year. Their task was then to restore order after a day of violence following the forcible break-up of a marathon demonstration in University Square. The demonstration began on April 22, 1990, as a peaceful protest against the predominance of former Communists in the new regime and the lack of answers to the many questions regarding the mysteries of the revolution, the terrorists, and the *Securitate*. Several groups of participants at the December revolution, anti-Communist associations, and, a few days later, two students' unions – all independent of political parties – were among the organizers of the demonstration. After a brutal but unsuccessful attempt by the police to break it up in a predawn attack on April 24, the demonstration grew in size and significance. President Iliescu himself unintentionally helped it gain popularity by calling the participants "golani" (bums or vagabonds), a slur that the demonstrators turned to good and imaginative use, as a kind of title of nobility (they sang: "Better golan than party activist, better dead than communist").

I was on assignment in Bucharest during the demonstration's heyday in late April and early May, when up to 40,000 people gathered every evening in what was proclaimed "the zone free of neo-Communism," a perimeter flanked by the University of Bucharest, the National Theater, and the Intercontinental Hotel, where many died in December making the revolution. From a second-floor balcony on one corner of the university building, speaker after speaker, people of various political shades and social conditions, addressed the crowd. On the balcony and in the square were young and old, famous writers, actors, musicians, workers, students, prominent intellectuals, and some farmers. Slogans were chanted, songs sung, videocassettes played on a large screen, and Radio Free Europe's broadcasts carried live on the loudspeakers. An atmosphere of great excitement, noble dedication, and determination to speak up for true democracy prevailed during those unforgettable spring nights.

A short statement passed by the participants and repeatedly read from the balcony proclaimed the three goals of the demonstration: (1) all former members of the Communist nomenklatura should be barred for ten years from running for office (as provided by the "Proclamation of Timisoara" of March 11, perhaps the most important Romanian antitotalitarian manifesto); (2) legislation subordinating Romanian television to the political leadership of the country should be abrogated; and (3) the elections, set for May 20, should be postponed. "The great majority of us are the same who were on the street on December 21," the statement said. "We began then the struggle against communism. Now all we do is to continue it." They also sent an appeal to the "former ordinary communists" to join in the struggle for the ultimate abolishment of communism, stressing that they were, like all other Romanians, nothing but the slaves of party and *Securitate*.

None of the demands was accepted by the government. At one point in mid-May, while the election campaign was in full swing, Iliescu showed some flexibility, apologizing for calling the demonstrators "golani" and agreeing to a dialogue with their representatives. That dialogue never materialized, however, bogged down by minor details.

As the election date approached, attendance at the demonstration decreased and enthusiasm faded. With the election over, most of the supporting groups and associations, including the students' unions, withdrew. Tired and disappointed by the stunning victory of the National Salvation Front, the bulk of the demonstrators stayed home. Only the most radical of them still gathered in the square. They were apparently infiltrated by the police. The number of hunger strikers dwelling in tents in front of the National Theater – 62 at the height of the demonstration – shrank to a dozen. All they were still demanding was that an independent television station be authorized to operate. Most observers agree the whole movement would have died down in one or two weeks. The government suddenly lost patience, however.

In a predawn raid on June 13, hundreds of policemen took by surprise the 50 or so demonstrators still in University Square, among them a dozen hunger strikers. The police beat them, arrested most of them, and demolished the tents. Several crews started to clean the place and reopen it for traffic. Soon, however, hundreds of people gathered again on the streets leading to the square. There were clashes with the police. In the afternoon, the crowd managed to occupy the square and chase away the police. Then around 4:00 P.M. bands of dubious-looking young men set fire to the police trucks and cars that were blocking the square. Two hours later, the buildings housing the city police, the Interior Ministry, and the newly created Romanian Intelligence Service were set on fire or ransacked. The television station was also attacked by demonstrators and the broadcast interrupted for a couple of hours. During these assaults, the army and the police were all but nonexistent. Only by nightfall did the army appear on the streets of Bucharest, cooperating with the police in an effort to disperse the angry crowds and restore order.

As the streets were quieting down, Iliescu appeared on

television with an appeal for help to thwart "an attempt by fascist extremists to overthrow the government through violent acts." Early next morning, between 10,000 and 12,000 miners arrived in Bucharest from the Jiu Valley, 150 miles to the northwest. They were greeted in Victory Square by the president, who thanked them "for answering once again our call with working-class solidarity."[6] For two days they terrorized the city, savagely beating up scores of people, many without any particular reason, just because people looked suspect or were well-dressed. Armed with clubs, iron bars, chains, and sledgehammers, they attacked the university building, ransacking offices and laboratories, molesting students and faculty members, and arresting many of them, including the president of the League of Students, Marian Munteanu, one of the more articulate and charismatic leaders of the extraparliamentary opposition. Munteanu was severely beaten, admitted to the hospital with multiple fractures, then jailed for several months, and finally freed pending his trial on charges of incitement to violence. They also ravaged the Institute of Architecture, the headquarters of the main opposition parties, and the house of one of the opposition's presidential candidates.

Virtually all major opposition or independent newspapers, including *Romania Libera*, were forced to shut down. Several hundred people were arrested and kept in inhuman conditions for days, weeks, or months. Few of them were charged with any crimes. No evidence of a coup, fascist or otherwise, was ever made known. Before leaving, the miners, whose ranks were apparently well-packed with security agents, capped their exploit with a mini-pogrom in the Gypsy neighborhoods. The divisions within the Romanian society were immensely exacerbated. The civilized world was horrified.

There are still unanswered questions and unexplained circumstances regarding the violent outburst of June 1990. The parliamentary inquiry commission, appointed the same month, was not able to come up with a consensus report, issuing instead separate majority and minority documents after seven months of investigation. The two different reports, labeled "preliminary," gave contradictory versions of the events, the majority trying to exonerate the president and the government of any wrongdoing, but the minority placing much of the blame exactly there. The minority report generally confirms what many foreign and Romanian observers suspected – namely, that what happened in mid-June was a well-orchestrated operation, albeit gone wild at times, meant to intimidate and tame the opposition.[7]

In both the Romanian and foreign press, however, there was some speculation, based mostly on circumstantial evidence, suggesting that there might have been more than met the eye in those events – namely, some infighting within the power structure that was unrelated to the antigovernment demonstrations and that prompted Iliescu to bring the miners to Bucharest.

A Rift between the Army and the *Securitate*?

The suspicion of a rift relies generally on two premises: the apparent rivalry before and after the revolution between the army wing and the *Securitate* wing of the alleged anti-Ceausescu conspiracy and the asymmetrical fate of the two bulwarks of power. Some of the former conspirators spoke openly about the uneasiness, mistrust, and lack of cooperation between the two wings. Although the former army generals (and Silviu Brucan, who was allied with them) claim to have been instrumental in the victory of the revolution, it seems clear that they were the losers in the power games that followed Ceausescu's ouster. The army itself, however, despite its role in the shooting in Timisoara, Bucharest, and other cities during the uprising, came out mostly unscathed and with a feared mediating power, whereas the *Securitate* was at least theoretically disbanded and some of its high-ranking officers put on trial. These officers and others, as well as the publications that serve as their mouthpieces, have often attacked the army and demanded that army officers responsible for the killings during the revolution be brought to justice as well.

The army was always resentful of the preferred treatment given the *Securitate* by Ceausescu. Indeed, the army was poorly equipped and trained; it was used in construction and agriculture and controlled by the intrusive secret police. In the wake of the revolution, the army sought to take advantage of the strong popular sentiment against the *Securitate* to affirm its preponderance in the power structure. As we mentioned before, one version has it that the army staged the terrorist attacks to clear its reputation and appear as the savior of the revolution, while settling its accounts with the *Securitate*. After Ceausescu's demise, several bloody incidents were reported between the army and *Securitate* troops, both theoretically fighting on the side of the revolution and against the terrorists. The clashes were described officially as accidental but are believed by many to have been telling episodes of the feud.

Some Romanian and foreign analysts hypothesized that part of the heightened tension experienced by Romania during the summer of 1990 and later was a result of an escalation of the army-*Securitate* conflict. In any case, there is hardly any doubt that the new leaders were constantly preoccupied by the prospect of a military coup d'état. As early as two months after the revolution, Iliescu alluded in an interview with a French newspaper to the likelihood of such a coup in the event "chaos and anarchy" set in.[8] The subject came up on other occasions and was discussed intensely by the foreign press in the wake of the mid-June disturbances.[9] The Romanian president publicly chided both the army and the police for their inaction during the June 13 unrest, which, he argued, forced him to appeal for public (read: miners') support. Why was there no action from the two forces of order? The army suggested that its duty was to defend the country and its borders against foreign aggressors, not to intervene in domestic political quarrels. Additional hindrance came from a lack of legal regulations governing the use of the army on domestic missions and from the absence of the minister of defense, who was in Berlin for an international meeting at the time of the disturbances.

Much of the speculation concerning a possible military coup d'état was concentrated on the minister of defense himself. General Victor Stanculescu was a deputy minister of defense during the previous regime. The anti-Ceausescu conspirators said that they did not even approach him because of their fear of being exposed. They accused him of being with Ceausescu until the last moment and organizing Ceausescu's escape by helicopter because, they claimed, "he still did not believe the game definitively lost."[10] Stanculescu indeed ordered the helicopter to the Central Committee building on December 22 and saw the Ceausescus off from the roof of the building. The general explained that he was afraid of a violent reaction from the dictator's guards that would have made many victims in the event of Ceausescu's falling into the hands of the revolutionaries. "A helicopter resolved the situation and made possible the couple's trial," Stanculescu said in an interview.[11] Later he recalled the other three helicopters and left the dictator on his own. The general's role in Timisoara, where he was sent on December 17 in the team of high officials assigned to implement Ceausescu's order to fire on the people, is still unclear and at best contradictory. He must have had a commanding position both during the shooting and when the army stopped the operation and fraternized with the people (on December 20, two days before the same thing happened in Bucharest). Stanculescu apparently tried to avoid being involved anymore or having to report to Ceausescu about Timisoara by faking a bone fracture and having his leg put in a cast. He was called to Bucharest nonetheless, only a few hours before Ceausescu's flight.

In the immediate aftermath of the revolution, as head of the army, he was perhaps the most important element of power in the vacuum created by the dictator's ouster. As already noted, Iliescu mentioned the general's name in his first appearance on television on the early afternoon of December 22. Nevertheless, Stanculescu was not trusted by the new leaders, a distrust that must have been the reason why they appointed him minister of the economy and gave the Defense Ministry to General Nicolae Militaru. Stanculescu soon recovered his position as head of the military in early February, however, apparently at the insistent requests of the army. He seemed to have been quite popular among the military, a popularity that made him very powerful and fed the rumors of a coup that he strongly and emphatically denied. "I think that for Romania, that has known the consequences of two dictatorships and wants to become a part of Europe, any dictatorship, including a military one, is excluded," he said at a news conference in October 1990.[12] This denial did not put to rest the speculations regarding the general's personal ambitions, guesses fed, among other things, by some intriguing moves such as a visit he paid former King Michael in Switzerland.

Interestingly enough, at a certain point he seemed to enjoy the support of some of the younger officers. There has been a sizable movement in the army very actively trying to democratize the military. It organized several demonstrations in Bucharest and other parts of the country. One major organization belonging to this movement is the Action Committee for the Democratization of the Army. It was created shortly after the revolution and banned after the mid-June violence (being blamed for the army's inaction). All the indications are that it is still active. As for General Stanculescu, Prime Minister Roman shrewdly replaced him as minister of national defense with little-known General Nicolae Spiroiu in a government reshuffle in late April 1991. Stanculescu was given the precarious Ministry of Industry.

Although the army got the upper hand after the revolution, the *Securitate* is far from giving up. In fact, it seems to have engaged in a strong counteroffensive both behind the scenes and in the public arena, even though it does not exist officially. The public campaign waged in newspapers and magazines, some identifiable as mouthpieces of the former secret police, has two main objectives: first, to argue that most *Securitate* officers were patriots and compassionate men who had only the country's interests at heart, and second, to justify the perpetuation of the *Securitate* (albeit under a different name) after the revolution. The campaign took different forms, from defending *Securitate* officers and rewriting the history of the anti-Ceausescu uprising to elaborate essays on the need to continue (and even intensify) the espionage and counterespionage activities and keep under surveillance potential troublemakers. Investigative reports about questionable security operations or even a description of the internal organization of the (former) intelligence services of the Department for State Security were labeled as treason or denounced as illegal. All these efforts at rehabilitation seem to have the blessing of the new regime, as the National Salvation Front's newspapers often open their pages for articles, statements, and letters of this kind.

Back in February 1990, a new Romanian Intelligence Service (known by its Romanian initials as SRI) was created, headed by Virgil Magureanu, one of the principal anti-Ceausescu conspirators and closest to Iliescu. Magureanu was a professor at the Communist Party academy, but also held the rank of colonel in the *Securitate*. A coconspirator maintained that Magureanu joined the security police to plot more effectively against the dictator. But another plotter, former General Stefan Kostyal, alleged that Magureanu actually spied on the group of army generals who conspired separately to overthrow Ceausescu.[13] According to most accounts, Magureanu headed the *Securitate* wing of the conspiracy. Little else is known about him.

SRI officials said in October 1990 that 35 percent of the 15,324 former full-time *Securitate* officers had been rehired by the new service. Magureanu stated in an interview with a Western correspondent that all those employed were "carefully screened" to ensure they had not been involved in any crimes. A spokesman for the service told that same correspondent it was currently "investigating espionage, sabotage, terrorism and fraud."[14] The independent and opposition Romanian press has published numerous reports about known or suspected SRI agents being implicated in surveillance of opponents of the present regime. There is a widespread suspicion that the mail is still censored and telephone conversations monitored. People receive anonymous threats, feel they are followed, and have to deal with the same officers who made their lives miserable for many years.

Even people in high positions seem concerned by how the *Securitate*, its personnel, and its files are handled. A prominent personality in the front who requested anonymity told me in Bucharest that he fully trusted Iliescu but could not understand the way the president dealt with the *Securitate*. He suspected that Iliescu must have some debts to repay or promises to keep. Many Romanians have such suspicions, and some believe that the president might be, in certain subtle ways, a *Securitate* hostage.

Whichever version is true, the presence of the *Securitate* in its previous or its new incarnation poisons the political environment, maintains fear, encumbers the democratic process, and questions the genuineness of the change that occurred on December 22, 1989.

Give Me Liberty or Give Me Food

There is Eastern Europe, and then there is Romania. No sensible analysis of the Romanian Revolution of December 1989 and its aftermath can proceed successfully without this necessary separation. It is admittedly a paradoxical proposition because Romania has been a part of Eastern Europe geographically, historically, strategically, and politically for more than four decades. Still, it has traveled a road of its own in many respects, most notoriously by its early embrace of "national communism," by the kind of insane dictatorship it experienced, by the abrupt and bloody way it broke with dictatorship, and by the singular manner in which it chose to meet its immediate post-Communist future. Since the early 1960s, Romania has been rather consistently out of step with the rest of Eastern Europe. So it remains today.

Most revealing is the fact that Romania, alone among the former satellite countries, has elected recycled Communists as its top leaders. Ion Iliescu won 85 percent of the popular vote, and his National Salvation Front received 67 percent of the vote.[15] It was a crushing victory even if one allows for some fraud and rigging of the results. The Romanians were the only ones in the whole world to choose as president a former member of the party apparatus in free, internationally supervised elections.

One explanation is that most Romanians were inclined to view Iliescu less as a Communist and more as one who freed the country of Ceausescu and made quick and major improvements in their everyday lives. Indeed, immediately upon assuming power, the National Salvation Front filled the empty shelves of grocery stores, heated cold homes, lighted up the darkness of streets and apartments, and shortened the workweek. Many restrictive laws and regulations were abolished. Abortion was legalized; independent newspapers made their appearance; the practice of religion became possible; and passports were issued on request. These measures meant freedom to a majority of the population in a country deprived for so long of practically everything and where evil was so personified that the dictator's disappearance created the instant fantasy of deliverance.

In addition, the people were confused, hardly able to distinguish between different options, totally inexperienced in democracy, and fearful of the future. Close to 4 million of them had been members of the Communist Party; many had collaborated with the *Securitate*. Collaborators and their families may have totaled more than half of the population, "a nation of Dalmatian dogs" in which almost everybody was stained, as the joke went. These people felt more comfortable and secure with Iliescu and the front. The workers were told that unemployment and inflation would be avoided by a go-slow policy on economic reform. The peasants were frightened by the bugaboo of returning landowners' taking back their land.

An arsenal of rumors, manipulation, demagoguery, class and ethnic hatred, xenophobia, and fear was unleashed by the insecure front, with little regard for the moral and political health of a society that emerged ailing and dehumanized from more than four decades of totalitarianism. In March, violent clashes between Hungarians and Romanians in Transylvania resulted in several casualties and heightened ethnic tensions. An orgy of nationalism broke loose, with many ugly displays of traditional intolerance, from anti-Semitic slurs and vandalism to the already mentioned mini-pogrom against the Gypsies.[16] Although all this intolerance cannot be traced to the National Salvation Front, its responsibility in exacerbating friction and anxieties in society and the active participation of some of its press in the nationalistic frenzy place at least part of the blame at its door. An interesting fact has been the subtle courtship between the regime and certain right-wing extremist circles, at a time when President Iliescu loudly and repeatedly denounced alleged right-wing conspiracies to overthrow his regime violently.

An uproar of calumnies stifled the frail voices of the opposition parties, whose message did not reach the electorate or was not absorbed by it. These parties had limited access to the media, radio and television being controlled by the government and biased in favor of the National Salvation Front. The enormous proliferation of parties (82 ran in the elections) increased the confusion of the electorate and obscured the issues.

The nature of the main opposition parties has also dissuaded many voters. Unlike other former Communist countries where new, modern parties were created and made up the principal forces of the opposition, in Romania the old, prewar "historical" parties were resurrected and became the National Salvation Front's competitors. Their leaders were old and often gave the impression that they simply wanted to pick up where history left off before World War II and resume as though nothing had happened in the meantime. Moreover, the two opposition candidates for president returned from exile after the revolution. A fact that in other countries and circumstances could have been a plus was made into a handicap by manipulation of the distrust and mean envy of the long-suffering Romanians. The Liberal Party and the National Peasant Party, running separate and competitive campaigns, won a total of less than 9 percent of the popular vote, though their candidates for president did a little better, together winning 15 percent of the votes. (Remarkably these parties rank third and fourth in the Romanian Parliament, after the ethnic Hungarian Democratic Union.)

The frailty of the parliamentary opposition bolstered the importance of the extraparliamentary groups. Many young people and intellectuals felt little attraction for the parties, preferring to oppose the government independently. They took to the streets and grew into a more serious challenge to the power than the opposition parties. Some of the groups in which they organized themselves, such as the Group for Social Dialogue, the Independent Democratic Group, the Timisoara Association, the Students' League, the December 21st Association, and the independent trade unions "Fratia" (Brotherhood) are vigorous and influential. They represent, in the words of political scientist Vladimir Tismaneanu, "the germination form of the tender Romanian civil society." Tismaneanu wrote that "the awakening of the civil society will contribute to the flourishing of grassroots movements and groups whose role will be to exert continuous pressure on the government and permit citizens to experience genuine political participation."[17]

At the end of 1990, more cohesion developed between different segments of the opposition, with a trend toward unity as the political landscape began to change considerably in reaction to the worsening economic situation. Even the promise of limited prosperity dissipated into shortages, unemployment, skyrocketing prices, and poverty. The winter brought back the miseries of unheated homes and workplaces. The Romanian people seemed ready in May 1990 to settle for less freedom than the other people in the rest of Eastern Europe, provided their immediate needs were met. What they got in the following months was not even that little. Both freedom and food were in short supply and rationed. "At the price of one thousand dead, we regained last year's ration," a newspaper uttered in anger in August.[18]

The Economic Mess

Far from improving, the economic situation seriously deteriorated in virtually every respect after the revolution. It was a combination of a terrible legacy, political ineptitude, bad management, and a serious degradation of work ethics. As pointed out earlier, what the new rulers inherited from Ceausescu was an irrationally built and neglected industry, a ruined and depopulated countryside, ultracentralized economic management, and generalized corruption. The new regime, concerned more with its survival, did little to prevent deterioration and, in fact, contributed to it. Aiming at consolidating its power base, the new regime showed unconscionable largess to certain categories of workers and condoned a widespread relaxation of work discipline and production rigors. According to some estimates, during the first nine months of 1990, wages increased by roughly 40 percent, while production decreased by 30 percent. The decline in production was most severely felt in the energy field, where coal output fell 40 percent (while the miners obtained the steepest pay raises of all, obviously in return for their non-work-related services to the government). Workers' committees were allowed to choose the managers, who in turn acted, in the words of the minister of economics, "like union representatives." Rampant absenteeism, stealing, and black-marketeering became serious concerns. For the entire year 1990, industrial production amounted to only 77 percent of what it was in 1989; a further drop of 20 percent was registered during the first quarter of 1991. According to official data, in 1990 exports were down 42.1 percent and imports up 12.6 percent, with an annual trade deficit of $3.3 billion. On February 26, 1991, Prime Minister Petre Roman described the situation as a "deep economic crisis."[19]

Agriculture did not fare much better. Confusion reigned in the countryside about land property, individual plots, the fate of collective farms, marketing of produce, and use of machinery. In certain parts of the country, the peasants did away with the collective farms and parceled out the land among themselves. A new law concerning land ownership was passed in January 1991, aimed at restoring private property of farmland in most of rural Romania. It is expected that 70 percent of the farmland will revert to the peasants who owned it before the collective farms came into being or who actually tilled it. Critics found many shortcomings, some serious, liable to discourage the farmers from taking land into their ownership or likely to create great iniquities. Nevertheless, this law promises to radically transform Romanian agriculture and a large segment of the population in a very short time. According to the government, 1990 was a relatively good year in agriculture. A serious shortage of farmhands plagued the countryside, however, and the army was again called upon to help harvest the crops. The peasants' markets were better stocked, but the state-run grocery stores were virtually empty the whole winter.

For many precious months before the elections of May 1990, the new leaders, either by ideological restraint or for political gain, discouraged any serious talk about radical economic reform. They allied themselves closely with certain segments of the working class, those least interested in such reform and its likeliest casualties, while antagonizing various strata of the population most dedicated to change.

Moreover, they made an effort to discredit the very idea of privatization or foreign investment, strongly promoted by the opposition, by brandishing the horrors of capitalism, igniting xenophobia, and sounding the alarm that the country was about to be sold out to foreigners. The people were so confused that a poll found 4 in 10 Romanians equating privatization with privation. This confusion served the National Salvation Front well in the May election but gravely worsened the economic situation and inadmissibly delayed the urgently needed reforms. After the election, when such reforms could not be avoided anymore, there was no consensus and little understanding among the population about what the government had set out to accomplish. The mandate of the electorate, as shaped by the front's rhetoric, was exactly the opposite.

Nevertheless, the new government of young technocrats that Prime Minister Roman formed in the wake of the election simply took possession of much of the opposition's economic program and proceeded to implement radical reform. But the uncoordination, the resistance of the bureaucracy, the suddenness, and the lack of popular consensus made the exercise extremely rough and costly. The implementation began on November 1, 1990, with the painful liberalization of prices for most goods, which resulted in an instant price doubling and tripling. The Romanian currency, the leu, was devalued by 75 percent, but at one-sixth of the going unofficial rate it still remained far from achieving full convertibility.[20]

These first steps follow more or less the generally accepted scheme for a decisive transition to a market economy.[21] Ending excess demand and thereby the shortage economy may turn out to be more difficult in Romania than in other East European countries because of the lack of any private enterprise under the previous regime and the resulting highly monopolistic conditions, which have undergone very little change since the revolution. The private sector is emerging very slowly and reluctantly through a maze of legal and bureaucratic hurdles.

Because of specific economic conditions and the distinct political environment, the whole process of economic restructuring may encounter further barriers in Romania and impose a stiffer price on the population. There is little that can be patched up and a lot simply to shut down. Most of Romanian industry's giants sit on moving sand. Equipped with antiquated technology in a high degree of wear (imports of spare parts or new technology were restricted to a bare minimum during the long years of heavy debt repayment), they process expensive imported raw materials using imported energy to produce goods that are not competitive on foreign markets. The government's plan is to maintain for the time being these huge industrial invalids as some kind of public property; if it should want to privatize them, it is quite doubtful that anybody would want to buy them.

On the political side, the Communist bureaucracy is still much more powerful in Romania than in other East European countries because of the nature of the National Salvation Front as a refuge for former members of the party hierarchy. Although the government is remarkably free of the nomenklatura type of people and encompasses mostly young and competent technocrats, the rest of the power structure, especially at the local level, is strongly anchored in the old party and state machinery. Reports abound in the Romanian press about how the new decisions, laws, and regulations are being sabotaged by the bureaucracy at implementation. Perhaps the most serious political handicap of the present Romanian leadership, however, was until very recently its inability to attract international financial support vital for the economic transition.

On Probation

In December 1989, Romania gained the world's affection as never before. It soon lost it. The power of former Communists, the shadowy presence of the security police, the political and ethnic violence, the rough treatment of the opposition, and the government control of the radio and television all combined to undermine the postrevolutionary leadership's credibility abroad, especially in the West. In a few months, the precious capital of goodwill was mindlessly dissipated. One year after the revolution, Romania was the only East European nation yet to be admitted to the Council of Europe, excluded from Western economic aid, denied special treatment for its exports to the European Economic Community (EEC), and held at arm's length in the area of high-level diplomatic exchanges. It was still on probation.[22]

In early 1991, however, a significant change occurred with the admission of Romania as special guest in the Council of Europe and the decision of the Group of 24, which includes the United States and the main industrialized countries of the West, to make Romania eligible for economic aid. These steps were the first, albeit limited and conditional, recognition of Romania as an emerging democracy. Its status in the Council of Europe was still short of the full membership of other East and Central European nations — namely, Hungary, Poland, and Czechoslovakia. In fact, it belatedly reached the level of recognition that the Soviet Union had enjoyed for some time. Another significant step was made on March 8, 1991, when Romania was able to secure a $300 million loan coordinated by the Swiss-based Bank for International Settlements and involving the central banks of 11 Western countries, including the United States. All these prepared the ground for the first official visit to Bucharest by a Western head of state — French President François Mitterrand in April 1991. Mitterrand's trip almost coincided with Prime Minister Roman's private visit to Washington, marked by a cool reception from the U.S. administration.

Among Western powers, the United States was perhaps the most reluctant to engage the new regime in friendly cooperation. Although Washington was as enthusiastic about the Romanian Revolution as any other capital in the world, its suspicions were the strongest when some of the disturbing features of the new regime began to surface. Secretary of State James Baker III was the last Western high official to visit Bucharest in the wake of the revolution, and even then only for a couple of hours. At the inauguration of President Iliescu, which occurred shortly after the miners' violence of mid-June 1990, the U.S. ambassador was the only Western head of a diplomatic mission to boycott the ceremony. During the Children's Summit at the United Nations in October 1990, President Bush snubbed Iliescu, whom he met only socially, while going out of his way not only to meet officially with but also publicly praise all the other East European leaders. When Prime Minister Roman came to Washington in April 1991, Secretary of State Baker was the highest U.S. official to see him. Later, in June 1991, Vice-President Dan Quayle deliberately excluded Romania from his East European tour, while visiting all the other former Communist nations of the region. Like most of the other Western nations, the United States extended humanitarian aid ($80 million of it) but withheld from Romania long-term economic assistance and such valued rewards as MFN status.

The economic aid was badly missed. It could have made a difference in a country in so much need and so impoverished. Even more important, where governments are reluctant to direct their funds, private companies are less likely to invest. Foreign investments represent for Romania the only hope of emerging from its economic decay. There is little or no indigenous capital. Neither is there much enterprise, drive, or inventiveness so far. These qualities also atrophied during decades of communism. The general uncertainty and bewilderment are hardly conducive to the long-range planning and risk-taking that are prerequisites for meaningful investments of capital, either local or foreign. The legislation governing foreign investments is still relatively vague and unsatisfactory in such respects as the repatriation of profits. The government says it has received many offers from foreign investors. So far no major project involving investments in old or new industries has been announced. The process is bound to be slow and halting.[23]

Aside from Romania's trouble in the West, serious problems exist in its relations with neighboring countries. The ethnic violence in Transylvania severely strained its ties with Hungary. Environmental disputes and other bilateral problems worsened Romanian-Bulgarian relations. Several of the former Communist countries, Czechoslovakia in particular, strongly criticized the violent repression of the opposition. Developments in Bessarabia created delicate challenges between Bucharest and Moscow. The more aggressive approach that Moscow took in the rebellious republics, including Moldavia, heightened anti-Russian feeling in Romania. Numerous demonstrations were staged in support of the Romanian-speaking Moldavians and their defiance of Moscow. By the time of the union referendum in the Soviet Union, which the non-Communist government of Moldavia boycotted, large segments of the Romanian public were demanding the return of the former territory of Bessarabia (the main part of which forms the Republic of Moldavia) to Romania. "Jackboots out of Moldavia!" and "Russia is yours, Romania is ours"—such slogans became common and very popular. The Romanian government established close ties with the leaders of Moldavia but steered clear of anything that could be construed as territorial claims. The progovernment media and the National Salvation Front itself, however, went quite far and with little regard for diplomatic niceties.[24] Nevertheless, Romania was the first former Soviet bloc nation to sign a treaty of friendship with Moscow that commits the two countries to respect the inviolability of their borders and their mutual territorial integrity and makes no mention of the Moldavians. The treaty stirred controversy within Romania and criticism from other former Communist countries for the precedent it set on provisions such as those restricting some of Romania's security options.[25]

As far as the West is concerned, Romania is basically still on probation, and it may take much longer before the country fully breaks the wall of skepticism and suspicion. The Persian Gulf crisis opened unhoped-for opportunities for the Romanian government to make itself useful to the West, and it seized them quite astutely. A day before the Iraqi invasion of Kuwait, Romania took over the presidency of the UN Security Council, using it wisely and skillfully during the crucial first month of the crisis. That and its subsequent firm stand, including its cosponsorship of the pivotal resolution authorizing the use of force, brought it desperately needed recognition from the United States. The crisis, however, also caused large losses for the Romanian economy estimated at more than $3 billion, mostly in unpaid debt ($1.7 billion) and canceled contracts. Given that many of these losses were clearly inevitable, the diplomatic respectability the Gulf crisis brought is a net gain and may prove an invaluable asset in the future. The prerequisite of a turning point in Romania's ties with the West lies, however, in the domestic developments, in the credibility of the democratization process, and in the progress made toward stability, tolerance, and civility. So far the prospects are bleak.

The Only Solution Another Revolution?

There is a sense of desperation in Romania today. The naive belief that getting rid of a dictator and a dictatorship brings at least a decent life evaporated like drops of dew on a hot August day. Little suggests, however, that it was replaced by a realization that gaining freedom and making it work presuppose more than an uprising. Many Romanians simply lost any hope. Up to 800,000 people may have left Romania for good in the first eight months of 1990 alone, having settled or being in the process of settling in other countries.[26] Others, however, joined the militant groups of the opposition. One year after the December revolution, the streets in Bucharest and other cities reverberated with the chant: "The only solution another revolution." It reflected the feeling that the December revolution remained unaccomplished, entangled in a myriad of contradictions, obstacles, intrigues, lies, rivalries, ineptitude, and plain wrong-doing. The civic responsibility that the demonstrations revealed was quite significant in a country that had kept silent for so long under the previous regime. Yet, whether indeed a new revolution is needed to change things and move ahead is not at all clear.

Change is probably unavoidable anyhow. The government has no choice but to go ahead with its economic reform package. This is already causing great social dislocations. The National Salvation Front's electorate seems in an accelerated process of disintegration. The workers, hardest hit by the reforms, have started to desert the front and rely on increasingly militant trade unions. A poll taken in March 1991 found that only 31 percent of the electorate would still vote for the front.[27]

The National Salvation Front itself has been experiencing considerable internal dissent. Silviu Brucan had talked back in September 1990 about the need for "a head to fall." In a televised interview, he said that "the time has passed when the rulers stayed in power no matter what their performance was, irrespective of the results."[28] He definitely meant President Iliescu. In December 1990, rumors of the president's imminent resignation were widespread in Bucharest. Certain ministers distanced themselves publicly from Iliescu, adding to the speculation about a serious rift. Prime Minister Roman was said to be at odds with the president and positioning himself to take over the top job in case of a resignation.

Assessing both the accuracy and potential impact of such reports is difficult. Nevertheless, in October 1990, when I had met Mr. Iliescu in New York, I had found him defensive and somewhat resigned to whatever fate had in store for him. He gave me his often-repeated line that assuming power under the postrevolutionary circumstances was politically suicidal. When the first, much delayed Congress of the National Salvation Front took place in mid-March 1991, there was relatively little disagreement and no sign of an imminent major split. It overwhelmingly elected Prime Minister Roman as leader of the party and approved a program to re-shape the NSF into a social democratic party.[29]

The political environment may have been significantly altered by the resurrection of the Communist Party under a new name in November 1990. Headed by Ilie Verdet, former prime minister and close associate of Ceausescu, the new party may hasten the National Salvation Front's internal crisis and force it to define itself in more precise ideological and political terms than before. Whether the new/old party can attract a sizable segment of the electorate remains to be seen. With much disappointment and some nostalgia for the past reportedly manifest among certain groups, it would not be too surprising to see some of the front's voters take a step to the left. So far, however, no opinion survey has found any major political inroads made by this party.

A much more disquieting phenomenon at the time of this writing is the political ascendance of an extreme na-tionalist movement. It counts among its membership and leadership both Ceausescu loyalists and neofascist ele-ments and manifests itself as the most vocal segment of the political spectrum. Initially nonpartisan but closely allied with and manipulated by the National Salvation Front, the ultranationalist groups have been showing a clear inclina-tion to act independently of late, to the point of acquiring a distinct political identity. There are at least two parties of this persuasion, one of them—the Party of National Unity of the Romanians—preferred by 8 percent of the electorate in a March 1991 opinion poll. This is not much, but the political potential of the ultranationalists is perhaps better reflected in the 56 percent found by the same poll to sympa-thize with the virulently anti-Hungarian organization *Vatra Romaneasca* (Romanian Cradle).

Two trends bode well for the future, however. One is the steady advance of a sense of unity among the democratic opposition. Umbrella political organizations were formed in the fall of 1990; at least one of them, the Civic Alliance, which rallies most of the extraparliamentary groups, seems to have a sizable following. Since May 1991, several of its most prominent members advocate its transformation into a political party to tap its potential electoral appeal. (In the IRSOP poll of March 1991, 31 percent of the respondents expressed favorable opinions – "good" or "very good" – of the Civic Alliance.) The other trend is the growth and strengthening of the independent and opposition press. The emergence of strong, courageous, and penetrating daily and weekly publications is perhaps the most welcome development of the postrevolutionary period.

Radio and television are still controlled by the government, but they have been displaying occasional signs of independence. Although no private television stations have been authorized nationwide thus far, several local stations have started independent programming. A good deal of concern arose in the spring of 1991 when the government approved the draft of a law reportedly stating that "freedom of the press can be exercised only in conditions of correctness, loyalty and good faith."[30] The bill would have imposed stiff penalties, including jail terms of up to five years, for such "transgressions" as the "defamation of the president of Romania" or "insulting" the government. It created an uproar both within Romania and abroad, where it was seen as a serious step backward on the road to democracy. Under pressure both at home and abroad, the government rescinded it.

A new factor has added a certain fluidity and quite a bit of stir to the political scene since the end of 1990. This is the reemergence of monarchy as a viable constitutional alternative to the present front-dominated republic. Formerly a mostly historical figure, King Michael has become a hot political property in Romania.

King Michael was forced to abdicate at the end of 1947 by the Soviets and their Romanian underlings. He lived quietly in Switzerland for four decades, with occasional public pronouncements of little impact. In the moral confusion and political promiscuity of the aftermath of the revolution, the longing for a stabilizing anchor with the blessings of legitimacy and solid antitotalitarian credentials substantially raised the political relevancy of the former king. As one who opposed both the fascist dictatorship of Marshal Antonescu and the Communist push for full control of the country, King Michael might have provided the missing credibility of the democratization process and a guarantee of its irreversible nature. In the spring of 1990, he requested a visa for a short visit to Romania with the purpose of praying at his ancestors' graves on Easter. The government turned down his request on the grounds that his presence might have disturbed the preelectoral political landscape. At Christmas that same year he did not wait for the government's permission and just landed at Otopeni airport in a private plane. Immediately upon completing the arrival formalities, the former monarch, accompanied by his wife and two of his daughters, headed toward Curtea de Arges, the town where his royal ancestors are buried. Halfway to their destination, the king and his party were stopped, taken back to the airport, and put on a military plane.

This expulsion stirred trouble for the government while increasing the awareness of the Romanian public, which had been intensely brainwashed against the monarchy over four decades, about King Michael and his supporters. The main parties of the parliamentary opposition, as well as the Civic Alliance, which is the umbrella organization for the extraparliamentary opposition, advocate either the return of the king or a referendum on the issue. The public, however, is divided, with a sizable majority apparently against restoring the monarchy.[31] Nevertheless, King Michael remains a wild card in a dynamic environment.[32]

Political and economic change may very well come about without one more violent revolution. Still, another revolution is definitely needed in mentality and behavior. Many factors suggest a breakdown of social intercourse, of the work ethic, of normal human bonds and conduct. Tolerance and dialogue are still the exception rather than the rule. Too many people seem to be easy targets for extremist delusions, nationalistic furor, and various enmities. The social dislocations of economic reform may create an even more unstable social climate with opportunities for extremists.

In the short run, further danger, upheaval, pain, and uncertainty lie ahead. In the long run, however, the future has to be bright for Romania — a country of much beauty, of rich national resources, and of proud people. For all that it was or was not, the December revolution remains the turning point.

Notes

Chapter 1

1. For interesting insights into and ample analysis of this issue and the Ceausescu regime in general, see Trond Gilberg, *Nationalism and Communism in Romania: The Rise and Fall of Ceausescu's Personal Dictatorship* (Boulder, Colo.: Westview, 1990); Freedom House, *Romania: A Case of "Dynastic" Communism* (Perspectives on Freedom no. 11, 1989); Mary Ellen Fischer, *Nicolae Ceausescu: A Study in Political Leadership* (Boulder, Colo.: Lynne Rienner, 1989); Vlad Georgescu, "Romania in the 1980's: The Legacy of Dynastic Socialism," *East European Politics and Society*, vol. 2 (Winter 1989): 69–93; Mark Almond, *Decline without Fall: Romania under Ceausescu*, European Security Studies no. 6 (London: Institute for European Defense and Strategic Studies, 1988); Walter M. Bacon, Jr., "The Liturgics of Ceausescuism," paper presented at the AAASS meeting, Boston, 1987; Vladimir Tismaneanu, "Byzantine Rites, Stalinist Follies: The Twilight of Dynastic Socialism in Romania," *Orbis* (Spring 1986): 65–69; Michael Shafir, *Romania: Politics, Economics and Society: Political Stagnation and Simulated Change* (London: Frances Pinter, 1985); Daniel N. Nelson, ed., *Romania in the 1980's* (Boulder, Colo.: Westview, 1981).

2. For comprehensive studies of Ceausescu's economic policies see, among other works, Serban Orescu, "Multilaterally De-

veloped Romania: An Overview," and Paul Gafton, "Romania's Socialist Agriculture: The Balance Sheet," in Vlad Georgescu, ed.,
Romania: 40 Years (1944–1984), Washington Paper no. 115 (New
York: Praeger/Center for Strategic and International Studies,
1985).

3. The following table shows the domestic increase in production and imports of selected raw materials and energy resources
between 1980 and 1988, as well as the percentage of imports in
the total quantity of each raw material or energy resource used by
Romanian industry in 1988.

	Quantity in Metric Tons (thousands)		Percent Increase	Imports Used as a Percentage of Total Resources, 1988
	1980	1988		
Iron ore				
Domestic production	1,460	2,252	54	
Imports	917	13,900	1,516	86
Coking coal (washed)				
Domestic production	994	3,608	363	
Imports	416	4,906	1,179	58
Metallurgical coke				
Domestic production	820	5,228	638	
Imports	656	1,099	68	17
Apatite concentrates				
Domestic production	0	0	0	
Imports	73	873	1,196	100
All fuels				
Domestic production	75,000	78,500	5	
Imports	30,600	44,100	44	35

Sources: A preliminary survey by the Romanian National Commission
for Statistics, February 1990. Ion Marcovici, "Ecuatia dezastrului" (The
equation of the disaster), *Romania Libera*, March 7, 8, 9, 1990; Petru
Pepelea, "Statistica la ora adevarului" [Statistics at the hour of truth],
Alternative, March 4–10, 1990, p. 26. The commission admitted that its
survey was based on incomplete data.

4. Ibid.

5. Ibid.

6. Professor Vladimir Trebici notes that during the harsh winter of 1985, the mortality rate grew by 22 percent compared to the normal rate for that time of the year, resulting in 18,000 more deaths. *Tribuna Economica* 8 (February 1990): 23.

7. World Health Organization data quoted by *Population Today*, March 1990.

8. Preliminary survey of the Romanian National Commission for Statistics, February 1990. According to the same source, the death rate in general was 10.7, compared to 8.7 in the United States.

9. *Washington Post*, June 7, 1990.

10. "Ted Koppel's Report," ABC News, April 2, 1990.

11. As we were told after the revolution, a conspiracy of some party members, mostly military men, had been in existence for more than a decade. Brucan was reportedly part of it. This conspiracy, however, will be examined in chapter 4.

12. Emigration, both legal and illegal, was widespread. The Jews were the first to leave. Close to 400,000 Romanian Jews settled in Israel, most of them in the first decades of communism. Legal emigration of Romanian citizens to the United States and West Germany picked up in the 1970s, in connection with the granting of Most Favored Nation status to Romania in 1975. According to State Department annual reports to Congress between 1975 and 1987, legal emigration included 132,979 to West Germany, 30,579 to the United States, and 18,471 to Israel. There were also many thousands of Romanian defectors to these countries and others.

13. Ingenuity was common to most dissenters. Radio Free Europe received letters and documents hidden in a doll, in a toothpaste tube, or in a candle, or written on silk sewn to the lining of garments.

14. Romania's foreign policy under Ceausescu is examined in such works as George Cioranescu, "Romania and Its Allies" in Georgescu, ed., *Romania: 40 Years*; Ronald H. Linden, *Bears and Foxes: The International Relations of East European States* (New York: Columbia University Press, 1979); and Aurel Braun, *Romanian Foreign Policy since 1965: The Political and Military Limits of Autonomy* (New York: Praeger, 1978).

15. Michael Shafir deals with this concept of "externaliza-

tion" of guilt and other features of the Romanian political culture in "Political Culture and the Romanian Revolution of December 1989: Who Failed Whom?" Jacques Rupnik, Pierre Kende, eds., *Culture politique et pouvoir communist* (Paris: Presse de la Fondation Nationale de Science Politique, forthcoming 1991).

16. For detailed analyses of U.S.-Romanian relations, see Robert Weiner, "The U.S. Policy of Differentiation toward Romania," David Funderburk, "Relations between the United States and Romania during the First Half of the 1980's," and Nestor Ratesh, "The Rise and Fall of a Special Relationship," in Paul D. Quinlan, ed., *The United States and Romania: American-Romanian Relations during the Twentieth Century* (Woodland Hills, Calif.: American-Romanian Academy of Arts and Sciences, 1988). See also, David B. Funderburk, *Pinstripes and Reds: An American Ambassador Caught between the State Department and the Romanian Communists (1981–85)* (Washington, D.C.: Selous Foundation Press, 1987), and Nestor Ratesh, "The American Connection," in Georgescu, ed., *Romania: 40 Years.*

Chapter 2

1. History as background for the Timisoara demonstrations of December 1989 is stressed in an essay by Romanian historian Victor Neumann published in *Orizont*, February 9, 1990, p. 4.

2. See Vladimir Socor, "Pastor Toekes and the Outbreak of the Revolution in Timisoara, *"Report on Eastern Europe* 1, no. 5 (February 2, 1990): 19–26.

3. Ibid.

4. "Explanation" by Laszlo Papp, bishop of the Oradea, Agerpress, December 21, 1989.

5. The vigil and the events that followed in Timisoara are abundantly documented in a valuable book of eyewitness accounts gathered and published by historian Miodrag Milin under the title *Timisoara 15–21 December '89* (Timisoara, 1990). The description of these events in the following pages is based on testimonies included in this book and in a more modest booklet by Florin Medelet and Mihai Ziman entitled, *O cronica a revolutiei din Timisoara* (Chronicle of the revolution in Timisoara) (Timisoara: Muzeul Banatului, February 1990), as well as on personal research and interviews.

6. A verbatim transcript of the meeting was published by *Romania Libera* on January 10, 1990.

7. Ibid.

8. Ibid.

9. This burlesque was initially included in the stenographic record of the meeting but then deleted the next day on superior orders. It was unveiled by an anonymous eyewitness in the newspaper *Adevarul* on January 14, 1990.

10. Hospitals confirmed receiving people wounded by firearms before 5:00 P.M.

11. Later some *Securitate* generals would claim that the destruction and looting were perpetrated by foreign agents to provoke bloody reprisals and turn the population against the army and *Securitate*.

12. *Romania Libera*, January 13, 1990.

13. An Oltean is a native of Oltenia, the region where Ceausescu was born.

14. According to the last survey of the East European Area Audience and Opinion Research (EEAOR) before the revolution, 63 percent of the adult population of Romania listened to Radio Free Europe. The share for the Voice of America was 31 percent, followed by the BBC with 25 percent and Deutsche Welle with 16 percent. EEAOR, *Listening to Western Radio in East Europe—1988*, July 1989.

15. *Romania Libera*, March 23, 1990.

16. The most detailed eyewitness accounts about the rally and what followed afterward were published during March and April 1990 by the independent newspaper *Romania Libera* in a long series of interviews and testimonies.

17. Radio Bucharest domestic broadcast, December 22, 1989.

18. *Romania Libera*, December 31, 1989.

Chapter 3

1. Interview with Petre Roman, *Le Monde*, January 5, 1990.

2. The recollections of Liviu Viorel Craciun, an early "minister of the interior," published in the Romanian magazine *Expres*, May 1990.

3. RFE monitoring of Radio Bucharest carrying live the television broadcast, December 22, 1989, 2:30 P.M.

4. Interview granted by Ion Iliescu to the French magazine *Le Nouvel Observateur*, May 17–23, 1990.

5. Ibid.

6. See Vladimir Socor's "The New President" in *Report on Eastern Europe*, no. 23 (June 8, 1990). Mr. Socor writes that "Iliescu remained on cordial terms with the Ceausescus throughout the 1970s."

7. As Vladimir Socor notes, Ceausescu himself was a Communist Youth leader in the immediate postwar period, and his son and heir apparent Nicu took over Iliescu's job as first secretary of Communist Youth Union and minister for youth affairs. Ibid.

8. *International Herald Tribune*, May 9, 1990.

9. *Le Figaro*, May 18, 1990.

10. Quotation from *Frankfurter Allgemeine Zeitung*, January 13, 1990. See Michael Shafir, "The Revolution: An Initial Assessment" in *Report on Eastern Europe*, no. 4 (January 26, 1990).

11. The video, which was never shown on Romanian national television, was one of the hottest documents shortly after the revolution. It was sold by unknown people to a French television station and played on New Year's Day. On January 2, 1990, the French newspaper *Liberation* published a transcript of the tape. During my stay in Bucharest in April and May 1990, the video was repeatedly shown in University Square, as part of the marathon anti-Communist demonstration there, and several Romanian newspapers published the transcript.

12. It is interesting to note that another of the six, namely Gheorghe Apostol, who was in the building and at one time knocked at the door and asked to be admitted to the room, was rejected. Later he would be accused by Brucan of cooperating with the *Securitate* after the letter was published and the signers were being harassed and repressed.

13. The name Civic Forum was obviously taken from Vaclav Havel's organization of that name in Czechoslovakia.

14. Interview published in *Expres*, May 1990.

15. The elections were later postponed under pressure from the opposition parties until May.

16. For a discussion on the number of casualties and the controversies it stirred, see page 78 of this book.

17. Lieutenant General Traian Dafinescu in an interview

with two reporters of the youth newspaper *Tineretul Liber*, March 27, 1990.

18. *Adevarul*, January 20, 1990.

19. *Adevarul*, August 23, 1990.

20. *Romania Libera*, August 25, 1990.

21. Petre Mihai Bacanu, "The Fifth Directory Accused of Treason?" *Romania Libera*, July 25, 1990.

22. Ibid.

23. *Romania Literara*, July 5, 1990.

24. Interestingly, this exchange was deleted from the (ostensibly verbatim) transcript of the interview published by the pro-government newspaper *Dimineata* on October 16, 17, and 18, 1990.

25. *Adevarul*, August 23, 1990.

26. *Baricada* 32, August 21, 1990.

27. Agence France Presse, December 31, 1989.

28. Radio Bucharest (in Romanian), February 2, 1990.

29. *Romania Libera*, September 28, 1990.

30. *Nouvel Observateur*, May 17–23, 1990, p. 47.

31. Ibid.

32. *Baricada* 32, August 21, 1990.

33. Sergeant Ion Enache's account in *Libertatea*, April 28, 1990. The Dimbovita county is close to Bucharest. The town of Tirgoviste is part of the county.

34. Radio Bucharest, December 23, 1989.

35. A tragic sequel to this trial was the March 1, 1990 suicide of the presiding judge, Gica Popa. There was much controversy about the meaning of this suicide; few doubted, however, that Judge Popa killed himself. In a short, handwritten letter, he explained that he could not find "another solution to free myself of fear and terror that would have made my life unbearable. . . . I don't reproach anything to anybody, I forgot them all." He also left a letter for his family. There were speculations and recriminations. In the end, everybody seemed to agree that depression and fear of retribution must have overwhelmed Judge Popa.

36. *Lumea Libera*, New York, June 16, 1990.

37. See, for instance, *Webster's New Collegiate Dictionary*.

38. Other cities included Sibiu – 93 dead; Brasov – 61, Braila – 40, Cluj – 26, Buzau – 25, and Tirgoviste – 13. The remaining 138 people were killed in other cities and towns. The figures were published by the Romanian press on June 10, 1990.

Chapter 4

1. Michel Castex, *Un mensonge gros comme le siecle. Roumanie, histoire d'une manipulation* (Paris: Editions Albin Michel, 1990).

2. Radu Portocala, *Autopsie du coup d'état Roumain: Au pays du mensonge triomphant* (Paris: Editions Calmann-Levy, 1990).

3. *Le Point*, May 21, 1990.

4. Portocala, *Autopsie du coup d'état Roumain*, 18.

5. Ibid., 26, 27.

6. *Romania Mare*, no. 14, September 7, 1990.

7. Anneli Ute Gabanyi, *Die Unvollendete Revolution: Romanien zwischen Diktatur und Demokratie* (Munchen Zurich: Serie Piper, 1990).

8. Interview broadcast on Radio Free Europe on July 19, 1990.

9. *Adevarul*, August 23, 1990.

10. See, for example, Marc Champion, "Romanian Revolution Depicted as Planned Coup, Not Uprising," *Washington Post*, August 24, 1990. The lead of this news story, datelined Bucharest, reads as follows: "The rule and life of Communist dictator Nicolae Ceausescu ended last December in a palace coup d'état that had been in various stages of planning since the mid-1970s, not in a spontaneous, popular uprising depicted by the government that replaced and executed him, two of the alleged plotters said today."

11. Radio Bucharest, January 4, 1990; and Reuters, January 4, 1990. As quoted in Michael Shafir, "Ceausescu's Overthrow: Popular Uprising or Moscow-Guided Conspiracy?" *Report on Eastern Europe*, no. 3 (January 19, 1990): 15–19. Michael Shafir pioneered the skeptical analysis of the available evidence regarding the alleged conspiracies, offering both the earliest and the best documented studies on the issue. See especially Michael Shafir, "Preparing for the Future by Revising the Past," *Report on Eastern Europe*, no. 41 (October 12, 1990): 29.

12. *Romania Literara*, July 5, 1990.

13. *Adevarul*, August 28, 1990.

14. In the Romanian Navy, Nicolae was a first-rank captain, which is a rank above captain and below rear admiral, corresponding to commodore in the U.S. Navy.

15. Indeed, Silviu Brucan would later doubt whether those

who wrote the letter actually lived in Romania, as they claimed. Interview with Italian Communist newspaper *l'Unita* as quoted by the Romanian newspaper *Romania Libera* on January 7, 1990.

16. For unknown reasons, the announced letter from the party academy was never received by RFE or by any other Western news organization. It should be added that it is now known that an important member of the group of conspirators was a professor at the academy.

17. *Adevarul*, March 30, 1990.

18. This remark was made in a personal interview with the cited person who requested that her name not be disclosed. Copies of the two letters are being kept in RFE's files. I proposed to meet with the purported author of the letters when he established indirect contact with us in late fall 1989, but he declined on alleged security grounds. At the time of this writing, he was still not ready to unveil his identity.

19. *Romania Literara*, July 5, 1990.

20. Jean-Paul Mari, "Le coup d'état qui n'a jamais eu lieu" (The coup d'état that never took place), *Le Nouvel Observateur*, May 17–23, 1990, Edition Internationale, pp. 46–47.

21. *Cuvintul*, February 1990.

22. *Cuvintul*, January 1991.

23. Ion Ionita was the head of the directorate with two deputies, Ceausescu and Corneliu Manescu. Manescu would also become an opponent of Ceausescu and one of the signers of the famous "Letter of Six" in early 1989.

24. Ion Mihai Pacepa offered the quoted comments in a personal interview in August 1990.

25. Ion Mihai Pacepa, *Red Horizons* (Washington, D.C.: Regnery Gateway, 1987), 194–195.

26. *Cuvintul*, January 1991.

27. *Adevarul*, August 23, 1990.

28. Silviu Brucan's books published in English include *Pluralism and Social Conflict: A Social Analysis of the Communist World* (New York: Praeger, 1990); *World Socialism at a Crossroad (New York: Praeger, 1987); The Post-Brezhnev Era* (New York: Praeger, 1983); *The Dialectic of World Politics* (New York: Macmillan, 1978); *The Dissolution of Power: A Sociology of International Relations* (New York: Alfred A. Knopf, 1971).

29. The interview was broadcast in three parts on RFE on September 6, 7, and 8, 1988.

30. Reuters, January 3, 1990.

31. *Report on Eastern Europe*, no. 3 (January 19, 1990): 18–29.

32. Ibid.

33. *Adevarul*, August 23, 1990.

34. *Scinteia*, December 21, 1990.

35. *Romania Libera*, September 8, 1990.

36. Playing prerecorded applause and cheers was a normal occurrence at rallies during the later years of Ceausescu's rule.

37. Gabanyi, *Die Unvollendete Revolution*, 21.

38. Pacepa, *Red Horizons*.

39. *Romania Libera*, May 12, 1990.

40. *Lumea Libera* (New York), no. 126, March 2, 1991.

41. *Lumea Libera* (New York), no. 127, March 9, 1991.

42. Ibid.

43. *East European Report*, no. 41 (October 12, 1990): 37.

44. Interview broadcast by Radio Free Europe on October 13, 1990.

45. *New York Times*, December 25, 1989.

46. Ibid.

47. During the quarter of a century of Ceausescu's rule, Bessarabia never became a major irritant between Moscow and Bucharest. Except for several historical studies published in relatively obscure magazines in the late 1960s, there were virtually no open challenges from the Romanian side on this issue: So much for Ceausescu's "nationalism."

48. For a closer look at how the Soviet media and officialdom dealt with the Romanian situation for most of 1989, see Dan Ionescu, "The Soviet Media's Inconsistent Attitude toward Romania," *Situation Report*, Romania/8 (November 1989), 3–7.

49. Western sources have been convinced that the withdrawal was initiated by the Soviets for their own reasons. The issue is amply discussed in Sergiu Verona, *Military Occupation and Diplomacy: Soviet Troops in Romania, 1944–1958* (Durham, N.C.: Duke University Press, forthcoming, 1992).

50. Michael Shafir, "The Revolution: An Initial Assessment," *Report on Eastern Europe*, no. 4 (January 26, 1990): 34.

51. Darie Novaceanu, editor of *Adevarul* and interviewer of Brucan and Militaru, wrote in an editorial published the same day as the interview: "My dialogue with them was much longer than it is published now. The details that are missing don't disturb the

entirety. I agree they would have enriched it with significant details. With very instructive scenes. With interesting projects — from simulators of gunfire bursts or helicopters' flights guided from the Adamclisi monument to a submarine that was supposed to abduct the dictator. And obviously with important absentees: many of those who took part or supported the conspiracy still keep for themselves their participation. They did not know each other, not all of them know (even now) each other. And it is good for a time to keep it that way." Darie Novaceanu, "Adevarul, Numai Adevarul . . . " [The truth, only the truth], *Adevarul*, August 23, 1990.

52. In a previous interview, Militaru said that he never told Iliescu about the military preparations.

53. This was the last question in the *Adevarul* interview of August 23, 1990: "When and where have you met for the first time? Answer: On December 22, at the television station and in front of the entire people. . . . "

54. Later, I asked the president whether the army and *Securitate* accepted him as leader absolutely spontaneously, with no prior deal. He replied: "No contact per se was established with anybody representing the Army or *Securitate*." That leaves open the possibility that there might have been talks with individual officers or with people representing parts of the two. Yet Iliescu denied even talking to General Stanculescu, the acting minister of defense, before giving his first televised speech on December 22. At least this denial can be proven wrong simply by reading the transcript of the speech in which he mentioned a telephone conversation with the general.

Chapter 5

1. The well-known Italian Communist leader Palmiro Togliatti himself once said that communism would be destroyed by former Communists. History did not prove him right, but many former Communists played a role in the demolition of the Marxist delusion.

2. *Expres*, February 23, 1990.

3. *Romania Literara*, July 5, 1990.

4. "22," February 2, 1990.

5. Some sources claim that during the January 12 demon-

stration Mazilu shouted with the crowd "Down with Iliescu" in a battle for power that he lost.

6. "22," October 26, 1990.

7. For detailed evidence, reporting, and analyses of the events of June 1990 and their aftermath, see Mihnea Berindei, Ariadna Combes, and Anne Planche, *Roumanie, Le Livre Blanc: La Realite d'un Pouvoir Neo-communiste* [Romania, the white book: The reality of a neocommunist power] (Paris: La Decouverte, 1990); Mihai Sturdza, "The Miners' Crackdown on the Opposition: A Review of the Evidence," *Report on Eastern Europe*, no. 2 (January 11, 1991); Michael Shafir, "The Parliamentary Enquiry into the June 1990 Events: Preliminary Conclusions," *Report on Eastern Europe*, no. 8 (February 22, 1991).

8. *Le Monde*, February 27, 1990.

9. The German press was especially interested in this topic. Here are, for example, two of the headlines: "A Putsch in Romania?" *Die Welt*, August 11, 1990 and "Rumors of a Putsch Augment Fear," *Koelnische Rundschau – Bonner Rundschau*, August 18–19, 1990.

10. *Baricada*, August 21, 1990.

11. *Revista de Istorie Militara*, no. 3 (1990).

12. *Romania Libera*, October 17, 1990.

13. See page 98 of this book.

14. Associated Press, October 17, 1990.

15. By comparison, in free parliamentary elections held in spring and early summer of 1990, the former East German Communists (with their party renamed the Party of Democratic Socialism) gained 16.5 percent of the votes, the Czechoslovak Communist Party 15.6 percent, and the Hungarian Socialist Party 8.5 percent. Even in Bulgaria, where the former Communists regrouped in the Bulgarian Socialist Party gained a majority, their share of the popular vote was 52.7 percent. See Charles Gati, "East-Central Europe: The Morning After," *Foreign Affairs* (Winter 1990–91), 129–145.

16. Charles Gati notes that touches of nationalism may be found in most of the former European Communist countries, although brandishing different symbols and cherishing different kinds of heroes. In Romania, the hero of choice is Marshal Ion Antonescu, the fascist dictator who led Romania into alliance with Hitler and was executed as a war criminal in 1946. Ibid.

17. Vladimir Tismaneanu, "The Revival of Politics in Roma-

nia," in *The New Europe: Revolution in East-West Relations*, Nils H. Wessell, ed. (New York: Academy of Political Science, 1991).

18. *Tineretul Liber*, August 21, 1990.

19. Address to the Parliament, February 25, 1991, quoted by the Romanian news agency Rompress, February 26, 1991.

20. Regular interbank currency auctions were introduced in February 1991 as a step toward full convertibility and a means to discourage what the Romanian press called "the dollarization of the economy," meaning the use of the dollar as an alternative currency on the domestic market.

21. See, for example, David Lipton and Jeffrey Sachs, *Creating a Market Economy in Eastern Europe: The Case of Poland*, Brookings Papers on Economic Activity, no. 1 (Washington, D.C.: Brookings Institution, 1990).

22. Freedom House in its comparative survey of freedom in 1991 still rates Romania as "not free," the only European country (aside from Albania) in this category. *Freedom around the World 1991, Freedom Review* 22, no. 1 (1991).

23. The government expects foreigners to invest at least $100 million in 1991. Whether this expectation is realistic remains to be seen.

24. A strongly worded resolution adopted by the National Salvation Front's Congress on March 17, 1991 expressed concern about tensions generated by the Soviet referendum and stated: "We are body and soul with our brothers in Moldavia." Reuters, March 17, 1991.

25. For an in-depth analysis of the Soviet-Romanian treaty, see Vladimir Socor, "The Romanian-Soviet Friendship Treaty and Its Regional Implications," in *Report on Eastern Europe*, no. 18 (May 3, 1991): 25–33.

26. This figure, announced by Radio Bucharest on September 2, 1990, was strongly challenged by the government. In light of more recent data it seems indeed an exaggeration. For an ample analysis of the postrevolution emigration issue, see Dan Ionescu, "Recent Emigration Figures" in *Report on Eastern Europe*, no. 7 (February 15, 1991): 22–24; and Dan Ionescu, "The Exodus," *Report on Eastern Europe*, no. 43 (October 26, 1990).

27. Rompress, April 9, 1991.

28. Interview on Romanian television, September 6, 1990. The transcript was published in *Cuvintul*, no. 11 (September 17, 1990).

29. Reuters, March 17, 1991.

30. Associated Press, March 12, 1991.

31. A public opinion poll conducted by the Romanian Institute for Public Opinion Surveys (IRSOP) in January 1991 found that only 13 percent of the sample favored the restoration of the monarchy and 18 percent wanted King Michael back. *Azi*, January 25, 1991. By March 1991, the percentage of those in favor of the monarchy rose to 17 percent, according to a poll conducted by the Independent Center for Social Studies and Opinion Polls. "22," May 4, 1991.

32. For more on the subject, see Michael Shafir, "King Michael's Second Expulsion," in *Report on Eastern Europe*, no. 3 (January 18, 1991): 21–25.

Index

abortion, 7, 142
accumulation rate, 4
Adevarul, 88
agriculture, 5–7, 146
Albania, 1
Andreescu, Gabriel, 13
anti-Semitism, 15, 143
Apostoiu, Dumitru, 54
Arab countries, Romanian workers
  in, 68
army: Ceausescu's escape and, 72;
  conspiracy against Ceausescu
  and, 85–86; democratization
  movement and, 139; Iliescu and,
  53; joining revolution, 34, 43,
  117, 118; new government discrediting, 62; operetta war and,
  62; postrevolution organizing
  and, 52–53; postrevolution power and, 136–41; reluctance in
  shooting and, 30; rivalry with *Securitate*, 136–41; shoot to kill order and, 27–31; Soviet assistance
  and, 112; terrorists and, 58

Babes, Liviu, 10
Bacanu, Petre Mihai, 62–63

Baker, James A., 112–13, 150
Banat region, ethnic diversity in,
  17–18
Bank for International Settle-
  ments, 149
Barladeanu, Alexandru, 54
Bessarabian issue, 113–15, 151
Blandiana, Ana, 13, 56
Bloody Sunday, 29–31
Bobu, Emil, 33
Botez, Mihai, 12
Brasov, 1987 workers' riots in, 10
British Broadcasting Corporation
  (BBC), 10, 11, 35, 83
Brucan, Silviu, 136, 153; Brasov
  riots and, 10–11, 99; Ceausescu's
  escape and, 71; conspiracy theories and, 85–87, 101–4; formation of interim government and,
  56; house arrest, 117; Iliescu
  and, 88, 99, 101; Letter of Six
  and, 11, 100; National Salvation
  Front and, 101; 1984 aborted
  coup and, 94; political career, 98–
  99; postrevolution politics and,
  100–101; Radio Free Europe interview, 99–100; Soviet knowl-

- Hora de la Prislop / Prislop Mountain
  Maramores District
    Festive Dance contest   2nd Sunday in Aug.
- Wine Harvest Folk Festival
  Tea
    500 year old Odo Basti Vinery
    Vrancea distr. last Sunday
    of Sept.
  - Sibiu Festival
    Sibiu / Medea. City Transylvania
    weekend of music and dance
      Sept.

- Musical Festival / Cluj- Napoca
    Transsylvania
    Musicians & Dancers celebr. change of
      seasons
    Nov.